China with enormous firepower and financial power fully capitalised on observing the lessons learnt from the Gulf War of 1991, and becoming the world's second largest economy. While at the same time, ensuring that it does not get involved in any war after the Sino-Vietnamese War of 1979, as it had a larger game plan, which neither the world including the USA could fathom until 2013, when Xi Jinping became the President of China. But by this time, China has galloped economically, militarily and diplomatically way past than anyone's expectations and estimations.

China with the combination of a single political party, no religion being discussed outside the four walls of a house, and plans & policies being implemented in a strict and stringent time frame has become a potent and powerful force that is ready to wage six wars in the next 39 years. The odds as on today are heavily in favour of China, winning these six wars that it will wage in Asia and the Indo-Pacific Region.

However, not all is still lost even as China's war clouds have started darkening. Strong and swift measures, if taken in a strict time frame can check China's checkmate. This book is an attempt to spread awareness of the China problem and solutions to solve this issue, that affects every global citizen in any country the world over.

CHINA'S WAR CLOUDS
The Great Chinese Checkmate

Lt Col JS SODHI (Retd)

BLUEROSE PUBLISHERS
India | U.K.

Copyright © Lt Col JS Sodhi (Retd) 2024

All rights reserved by author. No part of this publication may be reproduced, stored in a retrieval system or transmitted in any form or by any means, electronic, mechanical, photocopying, recording or otherwise, without the prior permission of the author. Although every precaution has been taken to verify the accuracy of the information contained herein, the publisher assumes no responsibility for any errors or omissions. No liability is assumed for damages that may result from the use of information contained within.

BlueRose Publishers takes no responsibility for any damages, losses, or liabilities that may arise from the use or misuse of the information, products, or services provided in this publication.

For permissions requests or inquiries regarding this publication, please contact:

BLUEROSE PUBLISHERS
www.BlueRoseONE.com
info@bluerosepublishers.com
+91 8882 898 898
+4407342408967

ISBN: 978-93-6261-457-5

Cover Design: Sadhna Kumari
Typesetting: Pooja Sharma

First Edition: August 2024

This book is dedicated to every global citizen committed to democracy and rules-based world order.

My immense gratitude to my family and friends.

Foreword

Admiral Karambir Singh, PVSM, AVSM (Retd)
24th Chief of the Naval Staff
Indian Navy

China's growing assertiveness, the ongoing great power confrontation and the resulting flash points in the Indo-Pacific coupled with the stand-off at the India China LAC portend that South Asia and the South China Sea will not remain peaceful in the foreseeable future.

Lt Col JS Sodhi (Retd) in his book "China's War Clouds: The Great Chinese Checkmate" has analysed the rise of China both economically and militarily. This according to him, coupled with its ever-deepening friendship with Pakistan, has emerged as a threat to the world order that can no longer be ignored; and we increasingly witness the manifestations of China's ambitions and intent around us.

The Author captures the essence of China, its geography, history, politics and leadership journey in a clear, concise and lucid manner with facts and figures; highlighting the gravity of the challenge that the world is confronted with.

The last chapter of the book details the steps that could be taken to contain and counter China and restore the rules-based order to an 'even keel'.

A go to book for not only professionals and defence enthusiasts but also for global citizens who wish to be initiated into the fascinating subject of China and it's rise.

My best wishes to Lt Col JS Sodhi (Retd) for this book and all future endeavours.

July 15, 2024

Author's Note

When I proceeded on premature retirement from the Indian Army on February 03, 2013, I had never fathomed that I would ever in my life be writing a book on any topic whatsoever. After my 21 years of service as a seventh-generation Indian Army soldier and a third-generation Corps of Engineers and a second-generation Bombay Sappers Officer, I had decided to work in the corporate sector for the balance of my life in the civil dress.

But strange are the ways of destiny and on December 09, 2021, I found myself in the field of media after I was requested by Nardeep Dahiya, the Editor of the reputed Indian publication *Firstpost* to write an article on a dear friend and my senior in school and the Indian Army, Brigadier LS Lidder, SM, VSM who had passed away a day earlier in a helicopter crash on December 08, 2021, in Coonoor,

For the next three months, I wrote general articles on the life and incidents in the Indian Army, until February 24, 2022, when Sanjeev Kumar of *India News*, a leading Indian news channel asked me to participate in a live-on-air discussion that was to be telecast just after 20 minutes at 11 pm that night on the Russia-Ukraine War that had broken out the same day.

Frankly, neither was I aware at that moment that Russia had invaded Ukraine earlier in the day, nor I knew any reasons leading to the outbreak of this war, but it was an opportunity and I did not let it go. I just spoke out of my military experience and after the discussion, thought that it was my first and last television appearance. However, it was not to be like I had envisaged. Thereafter, one news channel after the other started contacting me for debates and discussions, and print media publications started asking me for articles and comments on defence and geopolitical issues.

My interest in defence and geopolitics got rekindled, as the last time I had read any material on defence and geopolitical topics was for my Part D promotion examination in the Indian Army in 1996 as a young Captain at 25 years of age, and thereafter had shifted to the technical stream after doing my Master of Technology in Structures from the Indian Institute of Technology, Kanpur.

Being on numerous news channels and print media publications gave me an *on-the-job learning* experience and education, as I started reading more and more on defence and geopolitical issues. The reaction time given for either the electronic media or the print media appearances and articles respectively is very less, and one has got to be abreast with all the developments in the field of defence and geopolitics, since these two fields are very dynamic.

Apart from the credit for authoring this book going to 60 Indian and international news channels and 40 domestic and foreign print media publications on which I have featured, and numerous friends and family members guiding me in my initial days in the media, three people have been instrumental in the authoring of this book – Commodore C Uday Bhaskar, VSM (Retd), Brigadier TJK Ohri and Mahima Sharma.

Commodore C Uday Bhaskar, VSM (Retd), during a phone call in June 2022, told me to start making notes on every important topic I was giving my views on, as someday I would write a book. Honestly, I had not even thought of writing a book then.

Brigadier TJK Ohri, a good friend and course-mate, who guided me to write and update notes on a regular basis of any worthwhile defence and geopolitical happenings of the world.

Mahima Sharma interviewed me on China's threat to India which was published in *Indiastat*, a prestigious Indian publication on February 15, 2024. The interview received very good reviews from around the world. That day, I decided to write this book.

The next day on February 16, 2024, I started writing this book, and by the time I had completed it on May 10, 2024, the research I did for this book had me in awe and shock.

Awe, because there was so much information in the public domain about China's war clouds which the world at large was generally unaware of, and shock because there was so much less time left to contain China's checkmate.

And here is the book, *China's War Clouds: The Great Chinese Checkmate* which is the result of my research and reading. I am sanguine and sure that you, the reader, will find it equally interesting and informative as I did while writing it.

No research and reading in the world are ever complete, and I am certain that despite my best efforts and endeavour to include maximum information in the book, more can be added.

For it is in your and my hands to ensure that the checkmate of China is unsuccessful and the war clouds of China lighten, as there is no bigger victory than the victory of democracy and rules-based world order.

Contents

Topography of China 1

China's Tumultuous Formative Years: The Mao Zedong Era 7

China's Industrial Leap: The Deng Xiaoping Era 17

China's Rise as a Military Power: The Xi Jinping Era 28

The Taiwan War 67

War for Spratly Islands 92

Two-Front War on India 104

Countering China 146

List of Abbreviations Used 177

References 179

Index 185

1

Topography of China

Sun Tzu, a famous Chinese military strategist, quoted centuries back "Therefore, to estimate the enemy situation and to calculate distances and the degree of difficulty of the terrain so as to control victory, are virtues of the superior general".

Wars by a nation's army in the modern era are fought as a furtherance of the political objectives of the government of the day. Hence, it becomes important to understand why China is what today, and its assertiveness and aggressiveness. It is also imperative to understand the topography of China, for understanding its topography and terrain will throw answers to many questions that have remain unanswered about China.

China with an area of 95, 96, 960 square kilometres, is the third-largest nation in the world in terms of area, and its terrain varies from mountains to plateaus to deserts to plains.

China has a diverse landscape, with the Gobi Desert and the Taklamakan Desert in its north, and the Himalayas, Pamir, Tian Shan and the Karakoram Mountain ranges in its west. It has sub-tropical forests in its south, and a 14,500-kilometre coastline in its east.

The northern part of China primarily constitutes two big deserts – the Gobi Desert and the Taklamakan Desert. The Gobi Desert, has an area of 1.3 million square kilometres (500,000 square miles) is larger than the area of Germany and France combined. The Gobi Desert lies across northwestern China and southern Mongolia, is 1600 kilometres in length and 500-1000 kilometres wide. The Gobi Desert is rich in minerals and is divided into five distinct eco-regions viz. the Gaxun Gobi, Junggar Gobi and

Trans-Altai Gobi in the west; the Eastern or Mongolian Gobi in the centre and east; and the Alxa Plateau or Ala Shan Desert in the south.

The Taklamakan Desert is located in southwestern Xinjiang inside the Tarim Basin. The Gobi Desert lies on its east. The Taklamakan Desert covers an area of 337,000 square kilometres (130,000 square miles). The word "Taklamakan" is derived from the Persian word "Tark" meaning to *leave alone/abandon* and the Persian word "Makan" meaning *place*. The Taklamakan Desert's size is slightly less than Germany in comparative terms, and is 1,000 kilometres long and 400 kilometres wide. At its northern and the southern edge are two branches of the historic Silk Road. This desert has the distinction of being the world's second-largest shifting sand desert, as 85% of it is made of shifting sand dunes. The sand dunes in this desert range from a height of 60 feet (18 metres) to as high as 300 feet (91 metres). The Taklamakan Desert has a cold desert climate as it lies in the rain shadow of the Himalayas.

The western part of China has four main mountain ranges namely the Himalayas, Pamir, Tian Shan and the Karakoram ranges. The Himalayas are spread across five countries viz. Nepal, China, Pakistan, Bhutan and India, and have a total length of 2,400 kilometres (1500 miles). The Himalayas in India cover an area of 461,650 square kilometres, in Nepal cover 147,181 square kilometres and in Bhutan cover 38,394 square kilometres. The Himalayas in Pakistan extend about 320 kilometres (200 miles) into the country, with an area of 83,900 square kilometres. The Himalayas in China are located in the south of Qinghai-Tibetan Plateau and have an area of about 36,000 square kilometres.

The Pamirs are the most famous mountain convergence zone in the world, as they have been formed by the convergence of the Tian Shan Mountains, the Kalakunlun Mountains, the Himalayas, the Hindu Kush Mountains and the Jierter-Sulaiman Mountains. The Pamirs lie in the hinterland of Eurasia and extend across

China, Tajikistan and Afghanistan with an area of more than 100,000 square kilometres.

The Tian Shan Mountains, meaning "Mountains of God/Heaven" start from 400–600 kilometres (250 to 370 miles) east of Urumqi, north of Kumul City. The highest peak in this mountain range is Jengish Chokusu at 7439 metres (24,406 feet) and the lowest point is Turpan Depression, which is 154 metres (505 feet) below sea level.

The Karakoram range spans the borders of Pakistan, China and India with the northwestern extremity of the range extending to Afghanistan and Tajikistan. This range begins in the Wakhan Corridor, encompasses the majority of Gilgit-Baltistan and extends into Ladakh and Aksai Chin. The length of this mountain range is 500 kilometres (310 miles).

The southern part of China has sub-tropical forests. This area is called South China-Vietnam subtropical evergreen forests ecoregion, which covers the mountainous coastal region of southeastern China and northeastern Vietnam. This ecoregion also covers the coastal plains along the South China Sea and Hainan Island. Ecologically, the subtropical forests are at the northeastern extent of the Indomalayan realm. This ecoregion is mountainous for the most part, except along the coasts and around the Leizhou Peninsula.

The eastern part of China has a 14,500 kilometres coastline and is sub-divided into the northeast plain, north plain and the southern hills. The northeast plain extends north to the crown of the "Chinese Rooster" where the Greater and Lesser Hinggan ranges converge. The Changbai Mountains to the east separates China from the Korean Peninsula.

The North Plain is a large-scale downfaulted rift basin formed in the late Paleogene and Neogene and then modified by the deposits of the Yellow River. It is also the largest alluvial plain of China and is bordered to the north by the Yanshan Mountains, to the west by the Taihang Mountains, to the south by the Dabie

Mountains and to the east by the Yellow Sea and Bohai Sea. The Yellow River flows through the plain before its waters empty into the Bohai Sea. The part of the North Plain around the banks of the middle and lower Yellow River is commonly referred to as the Central Plain. The Central Plain is known as the cradle of Chinese Civilization and is the area from where the Han ethnic group of Chinese emerged. Beijing, the capital of China is located in the northeast edge of The North Plain. This plain also houses the other important Chinese cities like Tianjn, near its northeast coast, Jinan and Zhengzhou which are the capital cities of Shandong and Henan provinces respectively.

The North Plain is fertile and one of the most densely populated regions in the world, apart from being one of China's most important agricultural regions producing wheat, maize, sorghum, millet, peanuts, cotton and various vegetables. In the eastern part of the plain is also located the Shengli Oil Field. The North Plain is nicknamed the "Land of the Yellow Earth" due to yellow soil found in this region. The North Plain covers an area of 409,500 square kilometres (158,100 square miles), most of which is less than 50 metres (160 feet) above sea level.

The Southern Hills covers the area east of the Tibetan Plateau and fan out towards the Sichuan Basin, ringed with numerous mountains having 1000-3000 metres elevation. The floor of the Sichuan Basin has an elevation of 500 metres and is a densely farmed and thickly populated region. In the south of Sichuan Basin is the Yunnan-Guizho Plateau, known for its limestone karst landscape.

With this kind of a geographical layout, it is but natural that eastern China would be the centre of gravity of the country. No wonder eastern China is home to about 96.31% of the Chinese population and has the most important cities like Beijing, Jinan, Shanghai and Shenzen located in its eastern part.

Hence, the eastern part of China is the most vulnerable and China is aware that an attack on its coastline would make things difficult as it would get cut off from the world. It is this belly that is the most critical for China.

But to sustain eastern China, water is needed and since all rivers flowing in China emanate from the Tibetan Plateau, which is located in western China, its criticality assumes immense importance.

Tibetan Plateau, also known as the Qinghai-Tibet Plateau or the Qing-Zang Plateau, measures approximately 1,000 kilometres north to south and 2,500 kilometres east to west. It is the world's highest and the largest plateau above sea level and is surrounded by the world's two highest summits – Mount Everest and K2.

The Tibetan Plateau has in its midst the headwaters and drainage basins of all the ten major river systems of Asia. It also houses thousands of glaciers, thus serving as a "water tower" or a "water tank" to the 2.67 billion people living in Afghanistan, Ganga-Brahmaputra basin, southeast Asia and eastern China.

Tibetan Plateau is also referred to as the "Third Pole" as it holds the largest concentration of ice and glaciers outside the northern and southern poles.

This quite explains that, though Tibet declared its independence in 1913, China annexed Tibet after the Battle of Chamdo from October 06–24, 1950, in which 180 Tibetan soldiers and 114 Chinese soldiers were killed. China knows that the control of Tibet is important for its own existence.

China has been divided into 33 administrative divisions. They comprise 22 Provinces, 04 Municipalities, 05 Autonomous Regions and 02 Special Administrative Regions.

The 22 Provinces of China are Hebei, Shanxi, Liaoning, Jilin, Heilongjiang, Jiangsu, Zhejiang, Anhui, Fujian, Jiangxi, Shangdong, Henan, Hubei, Hunan, Guangdong, Hainan, Sichuan, Guizhou, Yunnan, Shaanxi, Gansu and Qinghai. China includes in its list Taiwan as the 23rd Province, which is an independent nation.

The 04 Municipalities of China comprise Beijing, Tianjin, Shanghai and Chongqing whereas the 05 Autonomous Regions are Tibet, Guangxi, Xinjiang, Inner Mongolia and Ningxia.

China also has two Special Administrative Regions, Hong Kong and Macau.

2

China's Tumultuous Formative Years: The Mao Zedong Era

Jin Meacham's quote "Without education, we are weaker economically. Without economic power, we are weaker in terms of national security. No great military power has ever remained so without great economic power" was perhaps followed in-depth by China, who rose from the ruins of a Civil War in 1949 and a poor country to a superpower in 2024. Such a dramatic rise within a duration of 75 years has not yet been witnessed in any nation in the modern era.

China with its immense economic power, military strength, nuclear arsenal and diplomatic clout has emerged as the third superpower of the world, the other two being USA and Russia. China's rise economically, militarily and diplomatically will be discussed in the subsequent chapters of the book.

After China was devastated by a civil war that ended in 1949, the literacy rate in China was just between 20–40%. The Chinese Communist Party (CCP), on taking over power made education as one of its foremost priorities, and through both formal schooling and literacy programmes was able to achieve school enrolment getting tripled, secondary school enrolment increasing by a factor of 8.5 and college enrolment quadrupling in the first sixteen years.

However, the next decade 1966–76, saw the Cultural Revolution in China which is formally known as the Great Proletarian Cultural Revolution. This was a socio-political movement launched by Mao Zedong, the founder of China and Chairman of the CCP, in 1966 and lasted until his death in 1976.

The stated goal of the Cultural Revolution was to preserve Chinese communism by purging the remnants of capitalism from the Chinese society. Though it ended as a failure in achieving its objectives, however the Cultural Revolution marked the return of Mao Zedong to the centre of power in China, as he had been sidelined by the moderate Seven Thousand Cadres Conference in the aftermath of the failure of the Great Leap Forward (1958–1962) and the Great Chinese Famine (1959–1961), during the currency of his chairmanship of the CCP.

The Great Leap Forward was launched by Mao Zedong as the Chairman of CCP in 1958 to reconstruct the country from an agrarian economy to an industrialised society through the formation of People's Communes. The People's Commune was the highest of the three administrative levels in the rural areas of China during the period 1958 to 1983, until they were replaced by townships. Communes, which were essentially large collective units, were in turn divided into production brigades and production teams. The People's Commune performed all the three roles of governmental, political and economic functions.

Mao Zedong decreed that efforts to multiply grain yields and bring industry to the countryside should be increased. Fearful of the decree and the Anti-Rightist Campaign (1957–59), the local government officials competed to fulfil or over-fulfil quotas as per the directives given, leading to the collection of non-existent surpluses, causing widespread starvation. This economic disaster was not reported up the higher chain of command, eventually leading to the Great Chinese Famine, in which an estimated 15–55 million people died, thus making it the worst famine in human history.

The Seven Thousand Cadres Conference, also known as the 7,000 Cadres Conference, took place in Beijing from January 11 to February 07, 1962, and was attended by 7,000 CCP officials nationwide. It is also one of the largest work conferences of CCP ever. The main aim of this conference was to deliberate and discuss the issues of the Great Leap Forward resulting in the disaster of the Great Chinese Famine.

In this conference, Chairman Mao Zedong made self-criticism in lines with the Marxist schools of thought, and subsequently took a semi-retired life, leaving the future responsibilities to the Chinese President Liu Shaoqi and Vice Premier Deng Xiaoping.

During the Seven Thousand Cadres Conference, probably for the first and only time in the history of modern China since 1949, did a senior Chinese government functionary admit publicly the failure of any of its policy. This happened when during the conference, Liu Shaoqi who as the President of China and Vice Chairman of the CCP, in a speech formally attributed 30% of the famine to natural disasters and 70% to man-made mistakes, as a result of the radical economic policies implemented during the Great Leap Forward.

After this historic conference, which saw Chairman Mao leading a semi-retired life, it was Liu Shaoqi and Deng Xiaoping who took over the mantle of running the government as well as the CCP. The conference also saw the correction of some far-left policies and institution of economic reforms like *Sanzi Yibao*, whose main highlights were free market and household responsibility for agricultural production. These reforms proved to be very beneficial to China, as time would reveal in the years ahead.

However, the Seven Thousand Cadres Conference also had serious divisions over who endorsed the *Three Red Banners*, which was an ideological slogan in China in the late 1950s which had called upon China to build a socialist state. The *Three Red Banners*, also called as the *Three Red Flags* consisted of the general line for socialist construction, the Great Leap Forward and the people's communes. The *Three Red Banners* was introduced in China after the first Five-Year Plan which was from 1953–57.

It was during the Seven Thousand Cadres Conference that, though Mao Zedong admitted to his mistakes in the Great Leap Forward, however gave a call to never forget the class struggle. This call would go on to become the base of The Cultural Revolution in China which lasted a decade from 1966 till Mao Zedong's demise in 1976.

However, Mao Zedong in a meeting in Beidaihe, which is a popular beach resort on China's Bohai Sea coast, in August 1962, said in a meeting that the class struggle must be talked about "every year, every month and every day". A month later, in September 1962, during the 10th Plenary Session of the 8th Central Committee of the Chinese Communist Party, Mao Zedong repeated his views on the class struggle expressed earlier.

Two years later in February 1964, Mao Zedong lashed out at the economic reforms being carried out by Liu Shaoqi going to the extent of calling the reforms as attempts to undermine socialist collectivism and to destroy socialism.

In 1966, Mao Zedong launched the Cultural Revolution, formally known as the Great Proletarian Cultural Revolution with the stated aim to preserve Chinese communism by purging the remnants of capitalist and traditional elements from the Chinese society.

The Cultural Revolution marked the return of Mao Zedong to active politics and power and lasted for a decade, until Mao Zedong's death in 1976. This period was one of the bloodiest eras of China in which an estimated 2 million Chinese died, though the real figures are not known and can be much higher. This period also saw the death of Liu Shaoqi in prison in 1969, who had been purged by Mao Zedong in 1967, apart from being labelled as "capitalist-roader", a Maoism term for a person or a group who demonstrated tendencies to bow to bourgeois forces and partake efforts to pull down the Chinese Communist Revolution.

This decade also saw the purging of Deng Xiaoping who in October 1969, was sent to the Xinjian County Tractor Factory in the rural Jiangxi province to work as a regular worker. Luckily, he wasn't physically harmed or imprisoned. Thus, both Liu Shaoqi and Deng Xiaoping who Mao Zedong had handed over power after the Seven Thousand Cadres Conference were removed from all constitutional and party appointments, which ensured that Mao Zedong had a free run after his return to power.

However, as time would reveal this was not to be.

Mao launched the Cultural Revolution in May 1966 after forming the Cultural Revolution Group (CRG) which was also known as the Central Cultural Revolution Group. The CRG consisted of staunch Mao loyalists, which included Chen Boda, Xie Fuzhi, Yao Wenyuan. Wang Li, Zhang Chunqiao, Kang Sheng and Jiang Qing (who was Mao's fourth wife) amongst others.

The CRG was so powerful that for some time it replaced the Politburo Standing Committee (PSC) and became the powerhouse of China. Though Chen Boda, a journalist and professor by profession, was chosen by Mao Zedong to head the CRG, but Chen Boda never addressed the CRG meetings. Rather Zhou Enlai, the first Premier of China from 1954 to 1976, addressed the CRG meetings.

August 1966 saw mass upheavals happening in Beijing. This month infamously came to be known as Red August which saw young people, mainly students, forming cadres of Red Guards throughout China. The *Little Red Book* was printed which was a compilation of Mao Zedong's select sayings. The *Little Red Book* was first published on January 05, 1964, and had widespread distribution during the decade-long Cultural Revolution.

The Cultural Revolution saw violence and chaos on an unprecedented scale in China, with the Red Guards on a rampage and a frenzy to destroy the Four Olds (old ideas, old culture, old customs and old habits). Large scale destruction of historical and cultural artefacts and religious sites was witnessed during this period. This period also saw the country's schools and universities being closed and the National College Entrance Examination being cancelled.

The Cultural Revolution was in essence divided into two parts – spring 1966 to summer 1968 (which saw the maximum death and destruction in China) and summer 1968 to 1976 (the period in which the Cultural Revolution tapered down till Mao Zedong's death).

The period 1966–68 also saw the Red Guards exhibit control over the People Liberation Army (PLA), apart from violent clashes happening in entire China.

In May 1968, Mao Zedong launched political purges on an unheard scale. A few months later on July 27, 1968, the Red Guards control over PLA was ended, and a year later in 1969, the Red Guards were dismantled totally as that time Mao Zedong felt that his political objectives of overthrowing those in powerful positions prior to May 1966, had been fulfilled.

April 1969 saw the 9th National Congress of the Chinese Communist Party, which was held in Beijing from April 01–24, 1969 in the Great Hall of the People, which is a state building located at the western edge of Tiananmen Square and had 1,512 delegates attending.

The 9th National Congress broke the ceiling set two decades earlier, in which rather through an election by party members, delegates for the 9th National Conference were selected by Revolutionary Committees. Also, it saw the election of more PLA members to the Central Committee, as high as 28%.

Premier Zhou Enlai announced in a grandiose manner, "We do not only feel boundless joy because we have as our great leader the greatest Marxist-Leninist of our era, Chairman Mao, but also great joy because we have Vice Chairman Lin as Chairman Mao's universally recognised successor".

Thus, the 9th National Conference was also the unofficial-coronation ceremony of Lin Bao. Marshal Lin Bao of the PLA played a pivotal role in the Communist victory during the Chinese Civil War from 1946–49. In the order of the Ten Marshals of PLA that time, Lin Bao ranked third, behind Zhu De and Peng Dehuai. Lin Bao was the Vice Chairman of the CCP from May 25, 1958 till his death on September 13, 1971. Lin Bao was also the Minister of National Defence from 1959 onwards until his demise.

Lin Bao was the first successor named in any communist government in the world and his name was written into the CCP constitution as "closest comrade-in-arms" and "universally recognised successor".

As China was engulfed in bloodbath and mayhem between 1966–68, it was also isolated internationally. This period also saw China becoming hostile to both the USSR and the USA.

Border clashes between China and the USSR increased significantly in March 1969 on the Ussuri River which is 897 kilometres long and runs between Khabarovsk and Primorsky Krais in the USSR and the southeast region of Northeast China.

As the war clouds between the USSR and China were getting darker by the day, the CCP decided in October 1969 to focus more on war preparedness than the internal situation in China. During this period, on October 18, 1969 Lin Bao issued an executive order to the eleven military regions of PLA to prepare for war. Since this executive order was issued without either the knowledge or approval of Mao Zedong, it jolted Mao who saw it as a direct attack on his authority.

As the frenzy increased in China for its war preparedness with the USSR, the popularity of Lin Bao grew exponentially, at the cost of Mao Zedong's stature.

While China was preparing for war, the factional rivalries within the CCP were increasing, which was quite evident during the Second Plenum of the 9th Congress of the CCP held in Luhan in August 1970. The PLA faction close to Lin Bao and led by Chen Boda, wanted the restoration of the constitutional appointment of the President of China, which was contrary to Mao Zedong's wishes.

Sensing greater problems within the CCP in the times ahead, Mao Zedong purged Chen Boda from the Politburo Standing Committee, whilst at the same time calling him a "false Marxist". Parallelly, Mao Zedong nominated several of his loyalists to both the Central Military Commission (CMC) and the Beijing Military Region, in order to reduce the clout of Lin Bao.

Clearly hurt and humiliated by these actions of Mao Zedong, which were reducing the powers of Lin Bao considerably, there was something being planned clandestinely in China, which would happen for the first and only time in modern China – a coup d'état.

Project 571 was the code word given by the supporters of Lin Bao, led by his son Lin Liguo, a senior ranked officer of the People's Liberation Army Air Force (PLAAF), of an armed plot to overthrow Mao Zedong as the Chairman of CCP and to then install Lin Bao as the Chairman of the CCP.

It was part of Project 571 that assassination attempts were made on Mao Zedong in Shanghai from September 08 to 10, 1971. It also included plans to bomb a bridge that Mao Zedong was to cross to reach Beijing. However, timely intelligence inputs made Mao avoid using this bridge.

Sensing the noose tightening around him, Lin Bao and his close family members and staff, which included his wife Ye Qun and son Lin Liguo, attempted to escape to the USSR in a Trident 1-E aeroplane on September 13, 1971. However, under mysterious circumstances the aeroplane crashed in Mongolia, killing all nine on board.

In the ensuing days and months, all Lin Bao loyalists were either arrested, purged or killed with a few lucky ones able to escape to Hong Kong, which was then under the control of the United Kingdom.

Lin Bao's incident had a serious impact on Mao Zedong's health and he became insecure, depressed and withdrew into a cocoon. Sensing helplessness, Mao Zedong reached out to his old comrades who he had purged in the past since the beginning of the Cultural Revolution a decade before. During all this inner restlessness, Mao Zedong appointed 38-year-old Wang Hongwen as the Vice Chairman of the CCP. Wang was a former factory worker with a farming background hailing from Shanghai.

Around the same time, Mao Zedong's wife, Jiang Qing started getting more politically ambitious and starting aligning herself more closely with Wang Hongwen, Zhang Chunqiao and Yao Wenyaun, who all together came to be known as the Gang of Four.

Zhang Chunqiao was a famous writer and a political theorist who had joined the CCP in 1938, whose article titled "Destroy the Ideology of Bourgeois Right" caught Mao Zedong's eye and the closeness between the two started.

Yao Wenyuan was a Chinese politician and literary critic, whose article "On the New Historical Beijing Opera 'Hai Rui Dismissed from Office" published on November 10, 1965 in Wenhuibao, launched the Cultural Revolution.

In 1973, the Chinese economy was in disarray due to focus on ideological purity over economic productivity. Zhou Enlai, the Chinese Premier, tried hard to restore the economy but the Gang of Four prevented him from working and constantly rebuked and resented him.

So much so that in late 1973, the Gang of Four launched a campaign called "Criticize Lin, Criticize Confucius" with the stated goals of purging China of the New Confucianist thinking and to denounce Lin Bao as a traitor. But the larger goal of this campaign was to discredit Zhou Enlai. Meanwhile, as luck would have it for the Gang of Four, Zhou Enlai was diagnosed with cancer.

This marked the return of Deng Xiaoping to active politics and he was named as Vice Premier in March 1973. Two years later, Zhou Enlai withdrew from active politics in January 1975 due to ill-health.

Deng Xiaoping's re-entry into active politics saw his meteoric rise at a breakneck speed which surprised many, especially the Gang of Four. In 1975, Mao Zedong made Deng Xiaoping the PLA General Chief of Staff, the Vice Chairman of the CCP and the Vice Chairman of the CMC, in addition to the post of the Vice Premier of China that he had assumed in March 1973.

The main reasons of Deng Xiaoping's meteoric rise were two-fold. One, Mao Zedong was using Deng Xiaoping as a counterweight to supress the loyalists of Lin Bao in PLA. And secondly, Mao Zedong had lost confidence in the Gang of Four but was unable to speak out openly for the fear of another coup d'état.

Zhou Enlai died of bladder cancer on January 08, 1976. Mao Zedong did not attend the funeral of Zhou Enlai. Little later on February 04, 1976, Mao Zedong appointed a relatively unknown Hua Guofeng as the next Premier of China. Hua Guofeng had joined the CCP in 1938 and had seen action in both the Second Sino-Japanese War and the Chinese Civil War as a guerrilla fighter.

On September 09, 1976, Mao Zedong died. As entire China plunged into grief and mourning, the Gang of Four was busy planning succession. Their radical ideas had already crossed roads with many party elders earlier, but the party elders could not do nothing till Mao Zedong was alive. With Mao Zedong's passing away was an opportunity presented and on October 06, 1976, the Gang of Four were arrested by the Special Unit 8341 of the Central Security Bureau on the orders of Hu Guofeng.

The era of Mao Zedong, which was turbulent and tumultuous, had come to an end.

3

China's Industrial Leap: The Deng Xiaoping Era

As the Chinese Civil War was raging, the Chinese People's Political Consultative Conference (CPPCC) was formed on September 29, 1949, just a few days before Mao Zedong would declare the creation of the People's Republic of China on October 01, 1949. The Chinese Civil War would end a few months later on December 07, 1949.

The CPPCC formulated the Common Program in 1949, which served as the interim provisional constitution of China till a written constitution was passed by the 1st National People's Conference in 1954.

Article 35 of the Common Program laid emphasis on the development of heavy industry so as to build the foundation for the nation's industrialization.

In furtherance to the Article 35 of the Common Program, China introduced Five-Year Plans since 1953, so as to steer the Chinese economy through detailed policies and guidelines which were to be followed in a time bound manner.

The First Five-Year Plan was from 1953–57, which had industrial development as the primary goal. The USSR provided full support to China in developing their industries from a scratch which saw lot of Soviet funding and experts being infused in China.

The First Five-Year Plan saw agriculture, fishing and forestry collectivized, and the government's control over the industry increasing by convincing the owners of the private firms to either sell them to the state or to convert them into joint public-private partnerships under the state control.

The First Five-Year Plan was successful to a great extent and China's industrial base expanded more than it was before the era of the Chinese Civil War. By 1956, China had completed its socialist transformation of the domestic economy.

The Second Five-Year Plan from 1958–62 saw increase in capital construction, industry, and income, as the industrial output doubled and the income of the farmers and workers increased by almost 30%. However, the Great Leap Forward which was launched during this period in 1958, saw millions of agricultural workers shift over into the industry, leading to substantial decrease in food production.

Such was the disaster of the Great Leap Forward that no Five-Year Plan was launched for the period 1963–65.

The Third Five-Year Plan, from 1966–70, laid stress on further development of coastal areas and more emphasis on consumer goods. This plan also for the first time in modern China's history, called for prioritisation of the national defence to thwart any possibility of a war.

The Fourth Five-Year Plan, from 1971–75, prioritised and decentralised labour intensive and small-scale developmental projects over capital intensive and large-scale development. It was during the currency of the Fourth Five-Year Plan that the visit of the US President Richard Nixon happened to China, a move that would boomerang badly on the USA and the World decades ahead. For, this move would help in China's meteoric economic rise, which would in turn propel China's military power. A deadly combination of economic, military, and nuclear power would unnerve many powerful nations and would thicken China's War Clouds, as it marked the beginning of the Great Chinese Checkmate.

China and the USSR saw gradual deterioration of their relations during Cold War 1.0, which was between the USA and the USSR owing to the doctrinal divergences on interpretation of Marxism-Leninism, were heavily influenced by external geopolitics and internal issues of the two communist nations. Essentially, Mao Zedong publicly rejected the USSR's policy of peaceful co-existence between the Western Bloc and the Eastern Bloc and also resented the USSR's closeness to India. The Sino-Soviet Split, as it would come to be known as lasted a decade from 1956–66, during which Mao Zedong severed all alliances and relations with the USSR.

After the end of the Chinese Civil War in 1949, the USA recognised the Republic of China (ROC) also known as Taiwan, as the sole government of China. However, as the Sino-Soviet Split was in force, the USA sensed an opportunity to get closer to the People's Republic of China (PRC) also called as China, with the main aim of down-cutting the might of the USSR.

Well before his election as the President of the USA in 1968, Richard Nixon had often hinted at establishing relations with China. It was with this aim in mind that, Richard Nixon's National Security Adviser, Henry Kissinger started working on this issue and flew on numerous secret diplomatic missions to China in 1971.

It was on July 15, 1971, that the US President Richard Nixon announced in a live televised address that he would visit China the next year.

The week-long historic visit by Richard Nixon from February 21–28, 1972, was the first ever visit by a US President to PRC, and it ended 25 years of no diplomatic relations between the USA and China. President Nixon described his week-long visit to China as "the week that changed the world".

Indeed, this visit would change the world in realms and reasons that one could have never imagined in that era.

The end of the week-long visit saw the issuance of the Shanghai Communique on the last evening of President Nixon's visit to China on February 27, 1972. The Shanghai Communique was issued after seven drafts were considered and reconsidered, included both the mutual interests of the USA and China as well as disagreements, with the latter being done on the suggestion of Mao Zedong, in order to create a more meaningful document.

The Shanghai Communique contained the US acknowledgement of all Chinese on the either side of the Taiwan Strait as One China, apart from including wishes of peaceful coexistence and expansion of cultural and economic contacts between the USA and China through bilateral trade.

Soon after the China visit, President Nixon found himself embroiled in the Watergate Scandal back home, which resulted in his resignation as the US President on August 08, 1974 and the US-Sino closeness slowed down.

Diplomatic relations between the USA and China were formally announced with the promulgation of the Joint Communique on the Establishment of Diplomatic Relations in 1979, in the presence of the US President Jimmy Carter and Deng Xiaoping during the visit of the latter to the USA from January 29–31, 1979. Deng Xiaoping's visit to America was the first visit by an important Chinese leader since the visit of Soong Mei-ling, the wife of Chiang Kai-shek, in 1943.

Present at the State Dinner in honour of Deng Xiaoping at the White House on January 29, 1979, was the former US President Richard Nixon, who had been invited specially on the request of Deng Xiaoping.

The Joint Communique on the Establishment of Diplomatic Relations ended the official recognition of Taiwan by the USA, and withdrawal of all US military personnel from Taiwan as the Sino-American Mutual Defence Treaty between Taiwan and the USA was absolved.

Thus, started the emergence of the People's Republic of China (PRC) as the new One China on the global horizon.

While all these geopolitics was being played internationally, Deng Xiaoping implemented the Four Modernisations Program in 1977, as a means of rejuvenating the Chinese economy in 1977. The Four Modernisations Programme was first announced by Zhou Enlai in January 1963, in Shanghai to work on the areas of Agriculture, Industry, National Defence and Science & Technology.

However, the decade of the Cultural Revolution from 1966–76 prevented the implementation of the Four Modernisations Programme.

Before 1977, the state-owned and collectively-owned enterprises represented 77.6% and 22.4% respectively of China's economic holdings. Deng Xiaoping realised that a strong manufacturing industry would propel China's rise as a world power. With diplomatic relations established with the USA and many other western European countries, China's international isolation was over.

Sensing a great economic opportunity that lay ahead, Deng Xiaoping set lucrative business terms for foreign investors and the process of attracting the foreign investors to China started aggressively. In-built Deng Xiaoping's economic vision's thought process was that, nations have to undergo urbanisation and a great deal of capitalism for a natural social transition. Also, the four core sectors identified under the Four Modernisations Programme namely, Agriculture, Industry, National Defence and Science & Technology would progress when China prospers economically.

For out of economic power, flows military power and eventually nuclear power. The three foundations on which a superpower nation is built. Deng Xiaoping was clear that China had to attain the superpower status one day.

The first major step undertaken by Deng Xiaoping was the creation of four Special Economic Zones (SEZ) on the southeastern coast of China: Shenzhen, Shantou and Zhuhai in the Guangdong province, and Xiamen in the Fujian province. These four SEZs were established in the period 1980–81.

Later on, the subsequent Chinese governments added three more SEZs in Hainan in 1988, Pudong in 1990, Binhai in 2009, and then eleven more were added, thus taking the SEZs to 14 more than the initial four planned.

The 3rd Plenary Session of the 11th Central Committee of the CCP which was held from December 18–22, 1978 in Beijing, saw the discussion and adoption of the "Reform and Opening Up Policy", which was mainly propounded by Deng Xiaoping, who is often called and credited the title of "General Architect" for the reforms that spearheaded China on the path of economic prosperity during the *Boluan Fanzheng* period.

Before the *Boluan Fanzheng* period and the further trajectory of China's economic prosperity is discussed, it would be prudent to delve on Deng Xiaoping's life journey, as he is the man credited the most for China's economic prosperity that would take the country on the path of being a superpower half a century later.

Deng Xiaoping was born on August 22, 1904, in Guang'an in Sichuan province. Deng's father, Deng Wenming was a graduate from the University of Law and Political Science in Chengdu and was a mid-level landowner.

Deng Xiaoping moved to France in 1921 as a teenager, where he studied and worked and slowly started getting influenced by the teachings and theories of Vladimir Lenin. In 1924, Deng Xiaoping joined the CCP and in 1926 he moved briefly to Moscow to study political science, before returning back to China in late 1927.

On his return to China, Deng Xiaoping joined the Red Army, as the military wing of the CCP was known during the period 1928–37 and became a Commissar, whose is responsible for the political education of the unit they are posted to, with the broader aim of ensuring political control of the military.

Deng Xiaoping played a prominent role during the Chinese Civil War that lasted from 1927–49, including taking part in the Long March from 1934–35, and China's war with Japan during 1937–45.

Along with Liu Bocheng and Chen Yi, Deng Xiaoping led the newly formed People's Liberation Army, which had been formed on October 10, 1947, into the Kuomintang capital of Nanjing during the final stretches of the Chinese Civil War in the latter half of 1949.

After the end of the Chinese Civil War, Deng Xiaoping had a meteoric rise in Chinese politics, starting with being the regional party chief of CCP for Tibet and southwestern China to returning to Beijing in 1952, and occupying a central position in the State Council as the Secretary General, which is the chief administrative authority and the national cabinet of China, under the leadership of Chairman Mao Zedong and Premier Zhou Enlai.

However, Deng Xiaoping fell out of favour of Mao Zedong during the Cultural Revolution and was purged twice during this decade.

Following Mao's death, Deng outmanoeuvred Hua Guofeng, who was Mao's chosen successor and became China's Paramount Leader during the 3rd Plenary Session of the 11th Central Committee of the CCP. This was the same meeting which saw the discussion and adoption of the *Reform and Opening Up Policy*, which was the brainchild of Deng Xiaoping. Paramount Leader in China is an informal term in Chinese politics for the most important political personality who controls the CCP as well the PLA.

Slowly but surely, Deng Xiaoping had established a grip on Chinese politics. This grip would propel China's economic growth and eventually its military prowess in the decades ahead.

Boluan Fanzheng was the period of far-reaching reforms carried out by Deng Xiaoping to correct the blunders of the Cultural Revolution, and is regarded as the inflection point in modern

China's history, which made China gallop at a breakneck speed economically, thus laying foundation for a strong military later.

This period also saw Deng Xiaoping correct the mistakes of the Cultural Revolution and restore order in China, which had seen immense chaos and mayhem during the Cultural Revolution.

The period of *Boluan Fanzheng* lasted up to early 1980s, after which the primary focus of the CCP shifted from class struggle to further modernisation and economic construction.

Now coming back to how the SEZs shaped China's economy.

The four SEZs created by Deng Xiaoping allowed them to be more lucrative and attractive to business, especially foreign investors. Tax and business policies were incentivized in such a manner that investment would flow in, that would create more industries and naturally employment too.

After the *Reform and Opening Up Policy* was propounded in the 3rd Plenary Session of the 11th Central Committee of the CCP held from December 18-22, 1978 the officials led by Yuan Geng in Guangdong province, prepared a blueprint for an investment project in Shekou for a ship-breaking facility. The plan was approved by Li Xiannian, a senior CCP leader, on January 31, 1979.

A few months later, in April 1979, Xi Zhongxun and few other Guangdong officials presented a broader plan for development of four cities in the coastal provinces of Guangdong and Fujian to attract foreign investment. The four cities proposed were Shenzhen, Shantou and Zhuhai in the Guangdong province, and Xiamen in the Fujian province.

When this plan was presented to Deng Xiaoping on July 15, 1979, he coined the term "Special Zones" for them and the four SEZs were officially established on August 26, 1979.

The Unique Selling Proposition (USP) of these four SEZs were business-friendly economic policies, low labour costs, robust infrastructure and the export-focussed businesses had the flexibility to respond to demand in foreign markets, which would give them more profitability.

The success of these four SEZs resulted in 14 more SEZs being formed, and thereafter the State Council started opening economic zones to its border areas along the Yangtze River and the inland areas, with more economic zones being opened up in the Pearl River Delta, Xiamen-Zhangzhou-Quanzhou Triangle, the Shandong and Liaodong Peninsulas, Hebei province and Guangxi region.

The State Council since 1992, has created 15 free trade zones, 32 state-level economic zones and 53 high-tech industrial development zones in various cities across the length and breadth of China.

Such was the success of the four initial SEZs that Deng Xiaoping remarked that the "SEZs were social and economic laboratories where foreign technologies and managerial skill could be observed".

This statement would have a great impact years later, when China would overtake the USA in many technical and technological fields, which at that time the USA would not have ever dreamt of.

Clearly, China was well on its track to be a superpower and in order to achieve this, it well understood the importance of technology.

Since inception, the SEZs have been the powerhouse of China's economic growth with the SEZs contributing 22% of China's GDP, 45% of total Foreign Direct Investment (FDI) in China and 60% of the exports.

The SEZs have created over 30 million jobs in China and increased the income of farmers by 30%. The per capita GDP of China in 1979 was a mere US$ 183.98 which has soared to US$ 13,160 in 2023.

The economic reforms that Deng Xiaoping ushered saw China having an average annual GDP over 10% for three decades.

Astonishingly, few years in this three-decade period saw the GDP over 13% annually.

The strong economic vision of Deng Xiaoping has resulted in China becoming the world's second biggest economy, just behind the USA in 2010 in nominal GDP terms and in 2016, China became the world's largest economy in Purchasing Power Parity (PPP) terms.

In 2023, China accounted for 16.9% of the global economy in nominal terms and 16.68% of the global economy in PPP terms, with China being the world's largest manufacturing economy and exporter of goods.

As of 2022, China stood second in the world in both the categories of having billionaires and millionaires, apart from having the world's largest foreign exchange reserves at US$ 3.1 trillion.

It is not that China had a rosy run towards economic prosperity. It has witnessed the 2008 Financial Crisis as well the 2023 Real Estate Crisis, however these brief economic downturns have not been discussed in this book because the net effect of these two economic downturns has been that China is still an economic powerhouse, which has neither affected its military, diplomatic or nuclear prowess.

Clearly, the economic policies and vision of Deng Xiaoping had veered China from Mao Zedong's staunch communist ideologies to foreign investments and technology, elevating a billion Chinese citizens out of extreme poverty.

It was but natural that the *Time* magazine named Deng Xiaoping as the Time Person of the Year for 1978 and 1985.

After an eventful political career that changed China's destiny, Deng Xiaoping died at the age of 92 years on February 19, 1997. As per Deng Xiaoping's last wishes, his body organs were donated for medical research and his ashes were scattered at sea.

Deng Xiaoping's view and vision that "development is the absolute principle", continues to shape China's governance till today, as

China was one of the few nations to have understood back in time that economic power was the bedrock of military, diplomatic and nuclear power.

4

China's Rise as a Military Power: The Xi Jinping Era

The quote of Sun Tzu, the famous Chinese military general and strategist "Ponder and deliberate before you make a move" is apt and appropriate for Xi Jinping, who waited in the wings before becoming the Paramount Leader of China in 2012 and eventually the President of China in 2013, before slowly unfolding his plans for China's military rise that would shake the world, including the USA, with its blitzkrieg of planning and execution.

Born on June 15, 1953 to Xi Zhongxun, a senior CCP leader who along with few other Guangdong officials, had presented the broader plan for development of four cities in the coastal provinces of Guangdong and Fujian to attract foreign investment to Deng Xiaoping, which would eventually be named SEZs and play a pivotal in China's economic prosperity.

With politics flowing in his blood due to the political lineage that Xi Jinping belonged to, he quite understood and planned China's upgrade to military might, as by then China was on a sound economic footing.

During the Cultural Revolution, Xi Jinping, as a teenager, was exiled to the rural Yanchuan County, in the city of Yan'an in the northeast of Shaanxi Province. It was during his exile that Xi Jinping joined the CCP after several failed attempts and was assigned the appointment of the local party secretary.

Subsequently, Xi Jinping studied chemical engineering in Tsinghua University, a reputed public university in Haidian, Beijing and then plunged full time into politics.

Xi Jinping was the Governor of Fujian from 1999–2002 and was thereafter made the Governor and Party Secretary of Zhejiang from 2002–2007. Meanwhile Chen Liangyu, was dismissed form the Politburo of the CCP in September 2006 for corruption in the Shanghai Social Security Fund and was later convicted in April 2008 for 18 years in prison for financial fraud and bribery.

Xi Jinping was appointed in the vacancy created by the dismissal of Cheng Liangyu in 2006 and elevated as the First-Ranking Secretary of the Central Secretariat, a year later in October 2007.

By the dint of his hard work and dedication, in a short time span in 2008, Xi Jinping was designated as the successor of Hu Jintao and as the next Paramount Leader of China, and was in the process appointed as the Vice President of China and the Vice Chairman of CMC.

On November 15, 2012, Xi Jinping was elected as the General Secretary of the CCP and Chairman of the CMC by the 18th Central Committee of the CCP.

On March 14, 2013, Xi Jinping was elected as the President of China replacing Hu Jintao. Xi Jinping is the first Paramount Leader born in modern China after the end of the Chinese Civil War.

The first two major decisions/initiatives taken by Xi Jinping after his ascendency as the Paramount Leader of China were the coining of the slogan *China Dream* in November 2012 and the *Belt and Road Initiative* (initially called One Belt One Road) in September 2013. These two major decisions/initiatives would play an important and integral role in China's rise as a military power which would happen in Xi Jinping's era.

The China Dream

Xi Jinping first coined the term *China Dream* during his visit to the National Museum of China in November 2012, after seeing an exhibit which was called the "Road to National Rejuvenation". Xi Jinping remarked that the *China Dream* is the great rejuvenation of the Chinese nation. This term soon spiralled as a slogan in China and started being extensively used in official announcements, and was strategically implemented keeping two important future events in mind – the centenary of the founding of CCP in 2021, and the centenary of the People's Republic of China in 2049.

In the widespread use of the slogan *China Dream* lay two important goals of Xi Jinping – one short-term goal and the other a long-term goal.

The short-term goal was the doubling of China's GDP from its 2010 level by 2020, which would encompass improving living standards and eradicating poverty, in order to achieve a moderately prosperous society.

The long-term goal being to enable China becoming a modern, prosperous, and strong socialist nation.

To make China strong militarily, Xi Jinping announced the *Belt and Road Initiative* during his first official visit outside China after being sworn as the President, to Kazakhstan in September 2013.

Two years later in May 2015, Xi Jinping promulgated the *Made in China 2025* policy that would further buttress China's rise militarily.

Let us analyse both the *Belt and Road Initiative* (BRI) and *Made in China 2025* policy in detail.

Belt and Road Initiative

During the first official visit of Xi Jinping to a foreign country after becoming the President of China, when he visited Kazakhstan on September 07, 2013, he proposed the "Silk Road Economic Belt" during a speech at Nazarbayev University in Astana, in which the Belt would include land routes for road and rail transportation through the landlocked Central Asia.

Next month in October 2013, during a visit to Indonesia, Xi Jinping proposed the "21st Century Maritime Silk Road", in which the term Road referred to the Indo-Pacific sea-routes through Southeast Asia to South Asia, the Middle East, and Africa.

BRI, which comprises both the "Silk Road Economic Belt" and the "21st Century Maritime Silk Road" has been propounded on the old trade routes that had once connected China to the West, undertaken by Marco Polo and Ibn Battuta in the ancient times and the maritime expedition routes of Zheng He, the famous admiral during the Ming dynasty that ruled China from 1368 to 1644.

The Belt and Road Initiative would include mega-investment infrastructure projects like ports, roads, bridges, railroad tunnels, dams and skyscrapers amongst a host of other infrastructure projects.

The aims and objectives of the BRI were for the first time officially presented in a document titled "Visions and Actions on Jointly Building Belt and Road", published in 2015. The document included six economic corridors, which, when implemented would enhance trade and investment. The flagship amongst these six economic corridors is the China Pakistan Economic Corridor (CPEC), which would have immense strategic and military implications aiding in China's rise as a military power, which shall be discussed later in this chapter.

The importance that BRI has for Xi Jinping and China's rise as a military power can be gauged from the fact that BRI was incorporated in 2017 in the Constitution of the CCP, which has 55 articles and was written in 1945 and formally adopted in April 1969 in the 9th National Congress of the CCP.

Though officially, the stated aim of BRI is to enhance regional connectivity and embrace a brighter future with the completion date being 2049, which will coincide with the centennial founding of the People's Republic of China. The unofficial and real aim of BRI is to aid in China's military rise, as sound infrastructure like roads and ports play an important and integral role in enhancing a nation's combat potential. This aspect hitherto hidden before, would slowly reveal itself as BRI would start progressing on ground in the years ahead.

According to various studies conducted by the World Bank, the BRI when completed will boost trade flows by 4.1% in the 155 participating countries, at the same time cutting the cost of global trade by 1.1–2.2%, and parallelly growing the GDP of the East Asian and Pacific developing countries in the range 2.6–3.9%.

The Centre for Economics and Business Research, a consultancy based in London, has said that BRI will increase the world GDP by US$ 7.1 trillion per annum by 2040 resulting in benefits that will be widespread, resulting in a frictionless world trade.

With such economic figures coming out in favour of the BRI by reputed international organisations, it is natural that as on August 2023, 155 nations out of the total 195 nations that exist, have signed up for the BRI. These 155 signatory countries of the BRI, include nearly 75% of the world's population and more than 50% of the world's GDP.

However, critics of BRI point out debt-trap diplomacy resulting in neo-colonialism and economic imperialism by China, apart from immense human rights violations and huge environmental impact, which are correct to a great extent

In 2023, a study carried out by College of William and Mary, Virginia, USA, pointed out that the BRI raised the probability of dual military and civil use and the ports being constructed under BRI will be favourable for future naval bases.

But for Xi Jinping, these criticisms don't matter as long as the BRI is aiding China's military rise, which it is in the cloak of bringing in global prosperity.

Now coming to *Made in China 2025* policy that further buttressed China's rise militarily.

Made in China 2025 Policy

Xi Jinping announced the *Made in China 2025* policy in May 2015, which is a national strategic plan and industrial policy with latent military aims that seeks to develop the manufacturing sector of China and in the process make China self-reliant in the sector of defence technology, which is a pre-requisite in a nation becoming a superpower.

Being the world's second largest economy since 2010, China decided to become a key player in the Fourth Industrial Revolution, which is technological advancement to include conjoining of technologies like artificial intelligence, gene editing and advanced robotics to blur the lines between the physical, digital and biological worlds.

Xi Jinping also wanted to overtake the USA in key technologies like artificial intelligence, aerospace, semiconductors, 5G, biotechnology, and electric vehicles so as to secure the domestic markets first and eventually capture the global markets, thus not only moving up China's manufacturing base higher up the value chain but having key defence technologies developed at home, ensuring no or little dependence on foreign firms for weapon systems whenever China decided to go to war. A strong and sound Military Industrial Complex plays the most crucial role in a nation's war waging capabilities as is evident in the case of the USA, and Xi Jinping was determined to make a sound Military Industrial Complex in China and *Made in China 2025* was an ideal policy to fructify this vision.

To ensure that the *Made in China 2025* policy is successful, Xi Jinping ensured state-funding of Research and Development (R&D), reduced taxation rates for the high-tech companies, incentivized mergers and acquisitions of foreign technology companies, ensured increased R&D funding by large manufacturers and set specific roadmap-targets for productivity and digitisation.

The following 10 key industries were identified in the *Made in China 2025* policy, most of which till 2015, were dominated by foreign players – information technology, robotics, green energy and green vehicles, aerospace, ocean engineering, railway equipment, power equipment, new materials, medicine and medical devices and agricultural machinery.

Also, to ensure the success of the *Made in China 2025* policy, Xi Jinping pumped in billions of dollars in form of R&D funding, tax breaks, interest loans and subsidies. Though the exact amount of money invested by China in the said policy is not known, but two pointers will well showcase the enormous amount spent by China for the success of this policy — US$ 2.9 billion for the Advance Manufacturing Fund, and US$ 20.2 billion for the National Integrated Circuit Industry Investment Fund.

Another big indicator of China's investment in the *Made in China 2025* policy is that as of beginning 2020, China had 200,000 5G towers, aiming to reach 5 million towers by the end of 2025. In the 14th Five-Year Plan, China earmarked US$ 1.4 trillion to build the 5G networks, which would also encompass installing cameras and sensors to create smart cities and their subsequent integration with the industry to accelerate mart manufacturing progress.

To further give fillip to the *Made in China 2025* policy, the *Thousand Talents Program* in vogue since 2010 which was an offshoot of the "Talent Superpower Strategy" launched in 2007, was rebranded as the *National High-end Foreign Experts Recruitment Plan* in 2019. The law enforcement and counter-intelligence agencies of the USA and other Western Europe countries were quick to label the *National High-end Foreign Experts Recruitment Plan* as a vector for intellectual property theft and espionage.

Also, part of the *National High-end Foreign Experts Recruitment Plan*, is the "Young Thousand Talents Program" which focuses on the recruitment of early career Science, Technology, Engineering & Mathematics (STEM) scholars.

STEM plays a pivotal role in development of indigenous defence technologies. For long, the USA had the world's largest PhDs (Doctorates) in STEM and hence the USA had a very sound and robust Military Industrial Complex, wherein the best and the latest defence technologies were produced in the USA since the largest number of PhDs in STEM were in the USA.

But all was to change soon.

In 2000, the USA produced 18,289 PhDs in STEM whereas China produced just 9038 Doctorates in STEM. But after the initial launch of "The Thousand Talents Program" in 2007 which also comprised "Young Thousand Talents Program", things started changing drastically in this field.

In 2010, China surpassed the USA in the number of PhDs in STEM, with China producing 34,801 STEM Doctorates and the USA producing 26,076. In 2019, the figures further soared to China producing 49,498 PhDs in STEM and the USA producing 33,759. In contrast, India produced about 700 PhDs in STEM in 2019.

By 2025, it is projected that China will have 77,179 PhDs in STEM, which will be nearly double of what the USA will produce at 39,959.

Now as the *Belt and Road Initiative* and the *Made in China 2025* policy started progressing on ground, Xi Jinping decided that it was time to usher in the Defence Reforms which when completed would aid and abet the *Belt and Road Initiative* and the *Made in China 2025* policy in China's rise as a military power.

2015 & 2024 Military Reforms

In 2014, something happened that the world took lightly, whose consequences it would pay later. People's Liberation Army (PLA) in its military doctrine stated that PLA is ready to fight any country anywhere in the world in all the six domains of war comprising: land, sea, air, cyber, electromagnetic spectrum and space. This declaration by the PLA was largely ignored by China's main adversaries like the USA and India, as that time the USA was still the undisputed solitary superpower in the world and under the wrong impression that no nation could challenge its status.

By the way, such a declaration hasn't been made any other military in the world till date including the US Military. Clearly, this was a trailer of the larger picture that lay ahead.

In fact, in the early 2000s, the popular joke in the corridors of Pentagon, the Defence Headquarters of the US Military, was that to cross the Taiwan Strait, the PLA will have to swim across it. Such was then the over confidence and the superior thinking of the US Military. The 2014 declaration of the PLA was taken lightly.

The PLA was founded on August 01, 1927, whose origins are traced to the left-wing units of the National Revolutionary Army (NRA) of the Kuomintang, against the nationalist government in the Nanchang Uprising. Then the PLA was known as the Chinese Red Army.

These two left-wing units comprising the Chinese Red Army were reconstituted as the People's Liberation Army in 1947. Since being reconstituted as the PLA, nine different military strategies called as "Strategic Guidelines" in China have shaped the PLA to its current form.

In 2004, the Paramount Leader of China, Hu Jintao, stated the following four missions of PLA –

- The insurance of CCP leadership
- The protection of the sovereignty, territorial integrity, internal security and national development of the People's Republic of China
- Safeguarding the country's interests
- Maintaining and safeguarding world peace

Ironically, the last point above of PLA's missions in maintaining and safeguarding world peace has today become the sole cause of worry for world peace as an aggressive and assertive China with enormous economic and military power, has its war clouds thickening, which would be discussed in due course.

The Central Military Commission (CMC) formed on September 28, 1954 is the highest defence organisation in China which comprises the PLA, the People's Armed Police and the Militia of China. Almost always, the Paramount Leader of China has been the Chairman of the CMC. The Chairman of the CMC is also the Commander-in-Chief of the PLA.

With the first two major decisions/initiatives by Xi Jinping, after his ascendency as the Paramount Leader of China, the coining of the slogan *China Dream* in November 2012 and the *Belt and Road Initiative* in September 2013 on the roll, the time was now ripe for the sweeping major restructuring reforms in the PLA, which would flatten the command structure and increase the combat potential of the PLA.

A year after 2014, when the PLA in its military doctrine stated that it is ready to fight any country anywhere in the world in all the six domains of war consisting of land, sea, air, cyber, electromagnetic spectrum and space, Xi Jinping announced China's Military Reforms in November 2015 at a plenary session of the CMC's Central Leading Group for Military Reform, which had been formed on March 15, 2014 under the stewardship of Xi Jinping.

The 2015 Military Reforms of China, saw the seven Military Regions of China that existed, regrouped and reorganised into five Theatre Commands, each would have: ground, air force, naval and rocket forces, which would enable each Theatre Command for enhanced combat potential and combat preparedness.

The CMC consists of four independent verticals comprising five Theatre Commands, four Services, four Arms and the Political Work Department. However, the operational roles of each of these four verticals is entwined.

The newly created five Theatre Commands of the PLA are – Eastern Theatre Command, Western Theatre Command, Southern Theatre Command, Northern Theatre Command and the Central Theatre Command. All the five Theatre Commands were formed on 1 February 2016.

We shall discuss each of the five Theatre Commands of China as they will play an important role in the wars that China will wage in the next four-decades.

The Eastern Theatre Command (ETC) with its Command Headquarters in Nanjing has its area of responsibility to include Fujian, Anhui, Shanghai, Zhejiang, Jiangsu and Jiangxi. The military focus of the ETC is East China Sea and the Taiwan Strait.

The Western Theatre Command (WTC) has the area of jurisdiction as Xinjiang, Tibet, Yunnan, Chongqing, Gansu, Sichuan, Qinghai and Ningxia. This is the largest of the five Theatre Commands of China and its military focus is India, South Asia, Central Asia, Pakistan & Afghanistan. The Command Headquarters are in Chengdu, Sichuan.

The Southern Theatre Command (STC) has the areas of Hainan, Hunan, Guangxi, Guangdong as well as the Special Administrative Regions of Hong Kong and Macau. It is headquartered in Guangzhou. Vietnam, Laos, Myanmar and the South China Sea are the primary military focus of STC, with amphibious operation against Taiwan being its secondary military focus.

The Northern Theatre Command (NTC) has its military focus on the borders with Russia, Mongolia and North Korea and the Sea of Japan, Yellow Sea and Bohai Bay. Its jurisdiction is Shandong, Jilin, Inner Mongolia, Liaoning and Heilongjiang, and its headquarters are in Shenyang.

The Central Theatre Command (CTC) is the smallest of the five Theatre Commands of the PLA with its headquarters in Beijing. Its primary responsibility being guarding the Chinese capital, and the secondary responsibility being training key personnel for leadership appointments for the numerous military academies. CTC is also the national strategic military reserve.

The four Services that are part of the PLA are: the People's Liberation Army Ground Force, People's Liberation Army Navy, People's Liberation Army Air Force and the People's Liberation Army Rocket Force.

The People's Liberation Army Ground Force (PLAGF) is the land-based service branch of the PLA which traces its origins to the Chinese Red Army from 1927, however, officially, the PLAGF was founded in 1948.

The People's Liberation Army Navy (PLAN), also known as the People's Navy or the PLA Navy, is the maritime service branch of the PLA and was founded on April 23, 1949. The PLA Navy is the biggest Navy in the world and has 370 warships and submarines and 380,000 personnel.

The People's Liberation Army Air Force (PLAAF), also referred to as the Chinese Air Force or the People's Air Force, is the aerial service branch of the PLA and was established on November 11, 1949. The PLAAF has a strength of 400,000 personnel and 3,510 aircrafts and helicopters.

The People's Liberation Army Rocket Force (PLARF), is the fourth service branch of the PLA and has in its arsenal conventional missiles of all types to include ballistic, cruise and hypersonic missiles, as well as nuclear missiles. PLARF was established on July 01, 1966, as the PLA Second Artillery Corps and its name was changed to PLA Rocket Force on January 01, 2016. It has a strength of 120,000 personnel. Its missile inventory is the largest in the world, comprising 1,200 short-range ballistic missiles, about 300 medium-range ballistic missiles, an unknown number of intermediate-range ballistic missiles, nearly 300 cruise missiles and 500 nuclear missiles.

The four Arms that comprise the PLA are the People's Liberation Army Aerospace Force, People's Liberation Army Cyber Force, People's Liberation Army Information Support Force, and the Joint Logistics Support Force.

The People's Liberation Army Strategic Support Force (PLASSF) was established on December 31, 2015 and was responsible for cyber, electromagnetic spectrum, space and political warfare domains. Its exact strength is not known, as it is the most secretive of the erstwhile five Service branches of the PLA and has many non-military personnel in its fold, apart from serving military personnel. On April 19, 2024 the PLASSF was disbanded and in its place the People's Liberation Army Information Support Force, People's Liberation Army Aerospace Force, and People's Liberation Army Cyberspace Force were raised.

The People's Liberation Army Information Support Force (PLAISF) has the responsibility of construction and implementation of joint information support to build a network information system that fulfils the requirement of modern warfare.

The People's Liberation Army Information Aerospace Force (PLAASF) will exercise command and control over the Chinese space forces, while the People's Liberation Army Cyberspace Force (PLACSF) will conduct defensive and offensive information operations, including reinforcing national cyber border defence, promptly detecting and countering network intrusions, and maintaining national cyber sovereignty and information security.

The Joint Logistics Support Force (JLSF) established on September 13, 2016 and was designated as an Arm of the PLA on April 19, 2024, is responsible for civil-military integration related to the logistics requirements of the PLA. The JLSF has established a Joint Support Big Data Centre, Theatre Joint Logistics Support Networks and Military Traffic Information Networks to support the efficient dispatch of the logistics units. The emphasis on a modern JLSF showcases the equal importance that the PLA accords to both the combat and logistics, both of which are quintessential in winning a war.

The fourth independent vertical under the CMC is the Political Work Department, which was created in January 2016 with its role to integrate the CCP and its ideology and propaganda in the PLA. The Political Work Department leads all the political and cultural activities in the PLA. For the promotion of any PLA officer or soldier, there is equal weightage in the annual assessment reports to both the military side and the political side. The political side's assessment is carried out by a Commissar of the Political Work Department who is posted at every level of formation, unit, and sub-unit of the PLA. Unlike most of the militaries worldwide where politics is kept separate from the military, in China, politics and military are an integral part of each other.

Alongside as the defence reforms were being contemplated by Xi Jinping, three important things were happening, which would in due course, play an equally important role in China's rise as a military power: enhancing its nuclear arsenal, enlarging the sea power, and the infrastructure development of Xinjiang and Tibet.

Enhancing the Nuclear Arsenal

China has come a long way from 1946 when Mao Zedong called nuclear weapons as a paper tiger in an interview to American journalist Anna Louise Strong in 1946, to a nation having the world's third largest nuclear weapons arsenal, with 500 nuclear warheads in its inventory as of 2023.

It was during the *First Taiwan Strait Crisis* in 1954–55, that the US President Dwight D. Eisenhower threatened to use nuclear weapons on China, that prompted Mao Zedong to commence China's nuclear programme, as he believed that by possessing nuclear weapons China would no longer be bullied and it would increase the diplomatic credibility too.

China with the aid of the USSR under President Nikita Khrushchev, began its nuclear programme in 1958, and subsequently conducted in first nuclear test in Lop Nur, Xinjiang on October 16, 1964, under a project codenamed as *Project 596*.

In 2013, when Xi Jinping took over as the President of China, there were 250 nuclear weapons in the Chinese inventory. This was far lesser than the 7700 nuclear weapons that the USA possessed, though more than double than the 110 nuclear weapons that India had. China has traditionally since 1949, treated the USA and India as its main two adversaries.

Realising the importance of nuclear weapons in its arsenal for both military power and diplomatic credibility— a lesson well-learnt from Mao Zedong— Xi Jinping tasked the China Institute of Atomic Energy, headquartered in Tuoli, near Beijing, to increase the nuclear inventory to 1000 nuclear weapons by 2030 and 1500 nuclear weapons by 2035.

Work on this directive by the Paramount Leader of China started in right earnest, and by 2023, China has 500 nuclear weapons, with the target timelines well within its capacity and capability.

The nuclear modernisation in China has ensured redundancy in delivery systems and better options for theatre nuclear strikes, be it by land, sea, or air.

China's main nuclear weapons arsenal includes the DongFeng (DF)-5A Intercontinental Ballistic Missile (ICBM), which is a single-warhead, three-stage and liquid-fuelled missile with a range of more than 13,000 kilometres. It also has DF-31 ICBMs with a range of 7,200 kilometres with three Multiple Independently Targetable Re-entry Vehicles (MIRV). Also in its inventory is DF-31A, an ICBM with a range of over 11,200 kilometres and six MIRVs. These ICBMs can easily target the cities on the US West Coast, either by direct launch or aided by aircrafts and submarines, as the distance between the West Coast of the USA and the East Coast of China is around 11,573 kilometres.

Approximately 55% of the nuclear weapons in China's inventory are in the medium-range category, with their main targets being regional theatre targets, which include Taiwan, India, Japan and the Philippines. This arsenal includes DF-3A and DF-21, which have an operational range of 5,000 kilometres and 1,770 kilometres respectively.

For the air delivery of the nuclear weapons, the PLAAF has 120 H-6s Bomber aircrafts, which can carry both nuclear as well as conventional missiles. China also has 270 Xi'an JH-7 Flying Leopard Bombers capable of undertaking nuclear strikes. PLAAF has also purchased 100 Su-30s (MKK and MK2 variants) from Russia, which can carry and deliver nuclear tactical weapons.

The sea-based delivery of the nuclear weapons, the PLAN has Type 092 Xia Class Sub-Surface Ballistic Nuclear (SSBN) submarines which are equipped with twelve JL-1 Submarine Launched Ballistic Missiles (SLBM), with a range of 2500 kilometres. JL-1 SLBM is a modified DF-21 missile. PLAN also has Type-094 SSBNs, which are capable of carrying twelve JL-2 SLBMs with a range of 14,000 kilometres. Work is also underway to complete Type 096 SSBNs by 2030, which would be fitted with JL-3 SLBMs with an operational range of 9,000 kilometres. China has six nuclear submarines (SSBN) as of 2023.

Enlarging the Sea Power

The quote by Sir Walter Raleigh, a British adventurer in 1829, "For whosoever commands the sea commands the trade, whosoever commands the trade of the world commands the riches of the world, and consequently the world itself", holds true today as it did almost two centuries back.

As explained in Chapter 1 of the book, the eastern part of China is the most important part, as the majority of its citizens and important cities lies in its eastern part. Also, on its eastern part across the Taiwan Straits, lies its most important military target, Taiwan.

To capture Taiwan, Xi Jinping realised that China has to have a formidable navy, as not only PLAN will play a pivotal role in the military operations for Taiwan, but it will also have to be formidable enough to take on the US Navy, which in 2013 was the biggest navy in the world, with 287 warships and submarines, while China had 273 warships and submarines in the same year.

Clearly, the numbers were grossly inadequate of PLAN to take on the might of the US Navy, and to deal with multiple maritime challenges like securing the South China Sea and the Malacca Strait Dilemma, in case China was to go to war with the USA over Taiwan.

Xi Jinping was clear that China's national maritime power had to step up if the *China Dream* was to materialise. Though the PLAN had surpassed the US Navy in size in 2015, but Xi Jinping was not contended with such statistics. In April 2018, Xi Jinping stated that "the task of building a powerful navy has never been urgent as it is today". China's 2019 Defence White Paper encapsulated the need for a modernised and strong navy that is capable of carrying out missions in the far seas. With this in mind, PLAN was told to construct two aircraft carriers, 21 nuclear submarines and 200 warships by 2030.

In comparison, 55 warships and submarines of the US Navy are under construction, while 67 warships and submarines of the Indian Navy are being constructed currently.

Work on constructing the warships and submarines started in right earnest in the six biggest and important shipyards of China: Bohai, Dalian, Jiangnan, Hudong Zhonghua, Wuchang and, Huangpu Wenchong.

The results were not only stunning but shocking too, as of 2023 the PLAN had by far surpassed the US Navy as the biggest navy in the world, but with a lead of 39 warships and submarines. The PLAN with 328 warships and submarines, is way ahead of the US Navy, with 289 warships and submarines. In contrast, the Indian Navy has 132 warships and submarines as of 2023.

By 2035, it is projected that China will have 430 warships and submarines which will include five aircraft carriers, whereas US Navy will have 355 warships and submarines, whilst the Indian Navy will have 175 warships and submarines.

It would be pertinent to highlight that arithmetically the number of warships and submarines in active service in China, the USA and India and those under construction will never add up, as some warships and submarines will be decommissioned owing to various factors like completing the service life or mechanical failures occurring, whose cost of repair and retrofit is much more than commissioning a new warship.

Between the period 2017 to 2019, China built more warships and submarines than United Kingdom, France, Australia, India and Japan combined. While the speed of construction of warships and submarines by China indeed has made the world gasp in awe and shock, the PLAN has kept its modernisation spree also focussed on its littoral warfare capabilities, with special attention to military operations in the South China Sea and the East China Sea.

China has been able to achieve the tremendous success in warship and submarine building by interestingly and ironically having joint ventures with Japan and South Korea, with whom its relations have subsequently soured due to their closeness with the USA.

In 2018, South Korea was overtaken by China to become the global leader in shipbuilding, and by 2020, the Chinese shipbuilders had captured 40% of the global market (by tonnage). The two biggest shipbuilding companies of China, the China Shipbuilding Industry Cooperation (CSIC) and the China State Shipbuilding Cooperation (CSSC) till 2019, constructed 75% of China's warships, submarines and merchant navy ships. In November 2019, both CSIC and CSSC merged into a single-entity called China Shipbuilding Group Cooperation, which has 21.5% of the global shipbuilding orders as of 2021.

Infrastructure Development of Xinjiang and Tibet

The western part of China, comprising Xinjiang and Tibet, are of critical importance to China as they border India, with whom China has frosty relations including a war in 1962, apart from an unsettled border which has often resulted in transgressions and intrusions. These include the *Galwan Valley Clash* in June 2020, ever since which the PLA and the Indian Army have been engaged in a standoff in the Ladakh region of India, which borders Xinjiang. Tibet's importance stems from the fact that Tibet is located opposite Arunachal Pradesh, an Indian state, over which China has staked its claim many times.

Thus, like enlarging PLAN's maritime power is essential for China, as its first and foremost military aim is to annex Taiwan, infrastructure development of Xinjian and Tibet too are of immense importance to China, as they will play a pivotal role when China attacks India for annexing Arunachal Pradesh.

Xinjiang and Tibet are two autonomous regions out the five such autonomous regions that exist in China for administrative purposes. Both these regions apart from being strategically important for China, also share a common similarity that these two regions were independent nations before China annexed them in October 1949 and October 1950 respectively.

Xinjiang, which was an independent nation by the name of East Turkestan before China annexed it in October 1949, is located in northwest China at an important location which is the crossroads of Central Asia and East Asia. Apart from being the largest subdivision of China, it is the eighth largest subdivision of any nation in the world. Xinjiang has an area of 1.6 million square kilometres and a population of 25 million people and borders India, Pakistan, Afghanistan, Russia, Mongolia, Tajikistan, Kyrgyzstan and Kazakhstan. Internally, Xinjiang borders the Chinese subdivisions of Tibet, Gansu and Qinghai.

Tibet, which existed as an independent nation by the same name before it was annexed by China in October 1950, covers much of the Tibetan Plateau as well as Mount Everest, the highest mountainous feature in the world. Officially called as the Tibet Autonomous Region (TAR), it has an area of 2.5 million square kilometres and a population of 3.64 million. Tibet borders the countries of Myanmar, India, Bhutan and Nepal and shares internal borders within China with the provinces of Xinjiang, Qinghai, Sichuan and Yunnan.

Thus, one aspect is clearly evident from the above, that had the world order led by the USA immediately post-World War II, prevented China from annexing both Xinjiang and Tibet, China would not have been as aggressive and assertive as it is today, as it would have been a much smaller nation, both in size as well as population.

A fatal error in judgement by the world powers decades earlier, will result in a higher price to be paid globally in the times ahead.

During the Chinese Civil War that ended in 1949, Mao Zedong sensing victory for the Communists started speaking of *Five Fingers of Tibet* in his various speeches stating that the *Five Fingers of Tibet* were China's responsibility to liberate and amalgamate in its folds. It is worth recollecting that during the Chinese Civil War, both Xinjiang and Tibet were independent nations which were subsequently annexed by China in 1949 and 1950, way after the Communists emerged victorious in the Chinese Civil War.

So, for Mao Zedong to mention about the *Five Fingers of Tibet* that considered Tibet as China's right-hand palm and five fingers as Ladakh, Nepal, Sikkim, Bhutan and Arunachal Pradesh (known as North East Frontier Agency then), clearly speak of the long-term strategic plans of China, which it always spells out in the public domain.

If the *Five Fingers of Tibet* were to be liberated, it was but obvious that first East Turkestan and Tibet, then independent nations were to be annexed soon after the Communists victory in the Chinese Civil War, which China eventually did.

Tibet was also very critical and crucial to China's existence because of one very important factor: Water!

Tibet, which houses the majority of the Tibetan Plateau, which is also known as the Qinghai-Tibet Plateau or the Qing-Zang Plateau, measures approximately 1,000 kilometres north to south, and 2,500 kilometres east to west. It is the world's highest and the largest plateau above sea level and is surrounded by the world's two highest summits – Mount Everest and K2.

The Tibetan Plateau has in its midst the headwaters and drainage basins of all the ten major river systems of Asia. It also houses thousands of glaciers, thus serving as a "water tower" or a "water tank" to 2.67 billion people living in Afghanistan, Ganga-Brahmaputra basin, Southeast Asia and eastern China. Tibetan Plateau is also referred to as the "Third Pole" as it holds the largest concentration of ice and glaciers outside the northern and southern poles.

To sustain eastern China, which houses an overwhelming majority of the Chinese population, as well as most of the important cities, water is needed, and since all rivers flowing in China emanate from the Tibetan Plateau, which is located in western China, its criticality assumed immense importance which was well understood by Mao Zedong.

But the global powers in the 1940s, be it the USA or the United Kingdom at that time, couldn't read and analyse China's strategic designs and thus remained a mute spectator when China annexed East Turkestan and Tibet in 1949 and 1950 respectively.

With East Turkestan (later renamed as Xinjiang) and Tibet finally annexed and amalgamated in the Chinese territorial limits, it was time to focus on annexing the other portions of the *Five Fingers of Tibet*, which lay in other foreign countries. But this was only possible if Xinjiang and Tibet had good infrastructure and with the poor infrastructure that existed in these subdivisions after annexation, it was near impossible for the PLA to reach the borders it had with India, Nepal and Bhutan.

But this was easier said than done. With a country fresh out of a civil war, China in 1952 had a GDP of US$ 30.55 billion and per capita GDP of US$ 54. With limited financial prowess, the Chinese policy makers decided to first concentrate on the development of eastern China for two reasons. One, the overwhelming majority of the Chinese population stayed in eastern China. Two, the priority one target for China to annex after the successful annexation of Xinjiang and Tibet, was now Taiwan. In fact, Deng Xiaoping famously remarked that "Let them (coastal China) get rich first, you (western China) can get rich later".

As eastern China prospered as the result of the US President Richard Nixon's visit to China, thus ending China's international isolation, and Deng Xiaoping's economic reforms started yielding results, it was time now for China to focus on its long-ignored and stagnated western part.

It was not that the western China did not see any worthwhile infrastructure projects in the first few decades after the Chinese Civil War. The construction of the Karakoram Highway, also known as Friendship Highway in China, was started in 1962 and was completed in 1978. This highway is a 1,300 kilometres highway connecting the Punjab province in Pakistan to the Xinjiang region in China.

Jiang Jemin, who was the third Paramount Leader of China from 1989 to 2002, proposed a developmental strategy for western China in March 1999 during the 9th National People's Conference. Further elaboration on this policy was done in June 1999, and the policy was officially named as the *Great Western Development Strategy* which is also many times referred to as the *Great Western Development Program*.

This policy covers the six Chinese provinces of Qinghai, Gansu, Shaanxi, Guizhou, Yunnan and Sichuan, all the five autonomous regions of Tibet, Xinjiang, Inner Mongolia, Ningxia and Guangxi, and one municipality Chongqing.

The *Great Western Development Strategy* covered 71.4% of mainland China's area, and covered just 19.9% of the economic output of China as of 2015.

The main highlights of the Great Western Development Strategy were development of infrastructure to include road and rail network, telecommunications and hydropower plants and energy and electricity networks. Emphasis was equally laid on encouraging foreign investment and reforestation, apart from educational enhancements and retention of talent in western China under this strategy.

The efforts of the *Great Western Development Strategy* propounded by Jiang Jemin, started yielding fruits, and by 2007, western China saw 92 key construction projects with an investment of more than 1.3 trillion yuan.

An integral element of this Strategy and also a part of the South-North Water Transfer Project, which is a mega infrastructure project that aims to channel 44.8 cubic kilometres of fresh water annually from the Yangtze River in southern China to the arid northern China through canal systems, known as the *Big Western Line*.

The *Big Western Line* is aimed at diverting water from the upstream sections of six southwestern China rivers to the dry areas of northern China through a network of tunnels, natural rivers, and reservoirs.

From 1999 to 2001, the western regions of Xinjiang and Guangxi reported an annual GDP increase of 30%, and all the western China's regions reported an annual average economic growth of 10.6% for six years in a row.

After Xi Jinping became the President of China in 2013, he quite well understood that the momentum of the development of western China had to be upgraded by a few notches in case his vision of the *China Dream* needed fructification.

The flagship project of BRI called the *China Pakistan Economic Corridor* (CPEC), was to pass through Xinjiang and apart from further boosting the trade and prosperity of western China, it would enhance the combat potential and combat power of the PLA, in unimaginable proportions.

The infrastructure development of Xinjiang and Tibet are slated to be completed by 2032.

China Pakistan Economic Corridor (CPEC)

The Malacca Dilemma, a term coined by the Chinese Paramount Leader Hu Jintao, has always bothered China as the sea route has traditionally and historically been the mainstay of oil and commodities for sustenance of eastern China. In the ancient times, both East Turkestan and Tibet were independent countries, and with the western region have a tough and rugged terrain, trade in huge magnitudes was near impossible. Hence logically and naturally, the sea route for trade became the most viable and cost-effective option.

But as China started getting economically strong and its military aspirations grew, it realized that the Malacca Strait, through which the majority of its trade happened, was also its biggest choke point. For if the Malacca Strait was blocked in the times of war, China would be rendered helpless for it's fuel and commodity requirements.

And conversely, was equally true in case of war that China can't export anything to the majority of its trading partner nations, if the Malacca Strait were to be blocked by China's adversaries. Whether for import or export, the important Shipping Lines of Communication (SLOC) for China pass through the Malacca Strait.

For 80% of China's oil imports and 90% of China's trade is through the Malacca Strait. Thus, the importance of Malacca Strait for China needs no over-emphasis.

The two main adversaries of China, both the USA and India have strong navies. Hence, apart from developing a strong maritime force, as has already been discussed in the preceding pages of this chapter, a viable alternate route had to be chalked out as a solution to the Malacca Dilemma, and the security of the Malacca Strait had to be undertaken.

The viable alternate route as the solution to Malacca Dilemma was to come in the form of CPEC and the security of the Malacca Strait was to be strengthened by way of *String of Pearls*.

As a precursor to CPEC, on May 23, 2013, the President of Pakistan, Asif Ali Zardari, and the Chinese Premier, Li Keqiang, agreed on enhancing mutual connectivity and developing a long-term plan for an economic corridor between Pakistan and China, during the visit of the Chinese Premier to Pakistan. Interestingly, during this visit, Li Keqiang was awarded Pakistan's highest civilian award, the Nishan-e-Pakistan. Clearly, this visit was as important to China as well as to Pakistan, as the turn of events in the years ahead would reveal.

This visit of the Chinese Premier to Pakistan was followed by two quick visits of the newly sworn-in President of Pakistan Mamnoon Hussien to China in February 2014, and two months later, the visit of the Pakistani Prime Minister Nawaz Sharif to China in April 2014 to take the economic corridor project ahead.

The visits of the top Pakistani leadership to China bore fruit, and in November 2014, China announced its decision to finance the US$ 45.6 billion energy and infrastructure projects in Pakistan, as part of this economic corridor.

On April 20, 2015, Xi Jinping visited Pakistan on his first state visit as the President of China.

Before embarking on the two-day visit to Pakistan, Xi Jinping authored an op-ed in Pakistan's Daily Times titled "Pak-China Dosti Zindabad" (Long Live the Pakistan-China Friendship), in which he wrote that "I feel as if I am going to visit the home of my own Brother" and also wrote that "the friendship between the two nations was higher than mountains, deeper than oceans and sweeter than honey".

On April 20, 2015, Pakistan and China signed an agreement to commence work on CPEC, on infrastructure projects worth US$ 45.6 billion during Xi Jinping's maiden state visit to Pakistan, setting the foundation for a strong and robust Pakistani–Chinese friendship with underlying military overtones, which China would many times call this relation with Pakistan as "Iron Brothers" and "All Weather Friends".

As part of CPEC, Pakistan would see a huge roads and rail network criss-crossing the entire country, linking the strategic seaports of Gwadar and Karachi in southern Pakistan to northern Pakistan, and further up to western China and Central Asia. The Karakoram Highway built in the 1970s would be totally reconstructed. A 1,100-kilometres-long highway would be built linking the two important cities of Pakistan, Karachi and Lahore. Also, the Pakistani rail network would eventually reach Kashgar in western China.

Apart from all this, CPEC also includes energy infrastructure under the *Early Harvest* scheme which entails creation of 10,000 Megawatts of electricity-generating capacity and a network of pipelines for transporting Liquified Natural Gas, wind-power projects, solar farms and the Hualong One nuclear power project near Karachi.

Eventually, with the subsequent addition of infrastructure projects the cost of CPEC has increased to US$ 65 billion.

India objected vehemently the CPEC project, as it passes through the portions Of Pakistan Occupied Jammu & Kashmir (POJK), which are an integral part of India but under the Pakistani occupation. However, China brushed aside the Indian concerns as this infrastructure web of CPEC was of vital importance to China, both economically as well as militarily.

As on January 01, 2024, 36 CPEC projects worth US$ 24 billion have been completed, and 22 projects valued at US$ 5 billion are in progress, and 26 projects of an estimated cost of US$ 27 billion are under negotiations.

Contrary to the public belief that CPEC is a failure, the statistics show that the implementation of CPEC is well on track to be completed by 2030.

When completed, CPEC will have dual civil-military use, apart from being an alternative viable trade route that solves China's Malacca Dilemma, CPEC will be used for military troop movement easily between China and Pakistan. Thereby, further enhancing the strong PLA-Pakistan Army ties that shall be discussed in detail in Chapter 7 of the book, and of course amalgamating the Pakistani-Chinese borders with India, called as the Line of Control (LOC) and the Line of Actual Control (LAC) respectively.

Xi Jinping through CPEC, effectively ensured the interlinking of the infrastructure development of Xinjiang and Tibet in western China to the important Pakistani military bases on eastern Pakistan, thus attempting to encircle India by the land-route.

It was now time for Xi Jinping to also solve the Malacca Dilemma through maritime means and also to entrap India by the sea route. And this was to be achieved through *String of Pearls*.

String of Pearls

The world's academicians and think tanks were correct in analysing that as China's economic power was growing and its military aspirations were rising, the only major geostrategic disadvantage it had was the Malacca Dilemma.

Booz Allen Hamilton, an US consulting firm with specialisation in intelligence headquartered in Mc Lean, Virginia, for the first time coined the term *String of Pearls* in 2004, which spoke of China's plans to expand its maritime power by building civilian maritime infrastructure across the Indian Ocean, which would have dual use by the military too.

The term *String of Pearls* subsequently found place in the US Department of Defence report titled "Energy Futures in Asia", published in 2005.

Pacific Forum researcher Virginia Marantidou, echoed similar views that China had anxiety regarding the naval blockade that could be imposed by the US and Indian Navies, by choking the Malacca Strait.

In 2008, David H. Shinn, an American diplomat and Professor of International Affairs at The George Washington University's Elliot School of International Affairs, expressed the Chinese need to secure the maritime supply lines from the Middle East and Africa to China.

It was not until the arrival of Xi Jinping on the Chinese political scene as the Paramount Leader in 2013, the work on the *String of Pearls* started in right earnest as a subset of BRI.

China proved the academicians and think tanks correct, when it signed the CPEC project with Pakistan on April 20, 2015 that included the development of Gwadar port. And not much later, China showed to the world that it meant business militarily when it opened its first overseas military base in Djibouti in 2017.

And soon thereafter, China acquired 85% stake in Hambantota International Port Group as part of its US$ 1.12 billion investment in the port, and taking the Hambantota port in Sri Lanka on a 99-year lease.

The *String of Pearls* had finally started fructifying and China's rise as a military power was happening at an unprecedented speed and unmatching scale.

China was surely and smartly securing the SLOCs through the various major maritime choke points in the Indian Ocean, such as the Strait of Hormuz, Strait of Mandeb, Malacca Strait and Lombok Strait by developing dual civil-military use maritime infrastructure in Horn of Africa as well as the littoral South Asian nations.

Though the construction of the strategically located Hambantota port began in January 2008 by China, it was in July 2017 that China got a 99-year lease to fully operate the Hambantota port after Sri Lanka expressed its inability to repay the debt it had taken from China. The Hambantota port is a deep-water port located in an important SLOC and is Sri Lanka's second-biggest port after Colombo.

Gwadar port in Pakistan, developed under the aegis of CPEC, part of the BRI, with a Chinese investment of US$ 1.62 billion, was formally made operational on November 14, 2016 and became fully operational on May 31, 2021.

On April 20, 2017, China got full rights to handle the operations of the Gwadar port for a period of 40 years. With this, China got an easy access in terms of the shortest-path to Africa, the oil-rich Middle East and Western Hemisphere, apart from the strategical advantage of overlooking the Arabian Sea, which is of vital military importance to India.

In March 2020, China started constructing a naval base for the Bangladesh Navy in Cox Bazar, which is located on the Bangladesh's southwestern coast, after having bagged a US$ 1.2 billion contract in 2017.

The naval base, christened as BNS Sheikh Hasina Naval Base, was inaugurated by the Bangladeshi Prime Minister Sheikh Hasina, on whom the naval base has been named, on March 20, 2023.

Two Chinese made Type 035G diesel-electric Ming-class submarines, which were purchased by Bangladesh from China in 2016 under the *Forces Goal 2030* military modernisation programme, are stationed in this naval base which has a total capacity of docking six submarines and eight warships simultaneously. PLAN officials have been sighted in this strategic

Bangladeshi port, which is in striking distance of India's eastern coast.

With full control over Pakistan's Gwadar port, Sri Lanka's Hambantota port and Bangladesh's Cox Bazar port, China's planning to entrap India by the sea route is complete.

And if this wasn't enough as a wake-up call to the world order about *String of Pearls* and China's aggressive and assertive rise as a global military power, reports started trickling in of China's infrastructure and, in turn, military activities in Kyaukpyu port located in Myanmar's Rakhine state.

Though as always, the official stated aim of China in developing any maritime or land-based infrastructure is trade and economy, the underlying and latent aim is always military use at a later date.

The same old trick has been used to justify China's investment in Kyaukpyu on the grounds that a world class deep-water port and free trade zone would not only allow the industries based in the Yunnan province of China easier access to the global markets through the Bay of Bengal, the Chinese investment of US$ 7.3 billion in this project would bolster the economy of Myanmar too.

Strategically, the development of Kyaukpyu port is a win-win situation as not only it too overlooks India's eastern coast but is also directly opposite Vishakhapatnam, which is the headquarters of the Indian Navy's Eastern Command.

The development of the Kyaukpyu port when completed would be a military masterstroke for China as it would be the nearest that the Chinese Navy can get to the either of the two operational commands of the Indian Navy, which are the Western Command and Eastern Command located at Mumbai and Vishakhapatnam respectively, as the distance between the Gwadar port in Pakistan to Mumbai is 878 nautical miles and the distance between Kyaukpyu to Vishakhapatnam is 793 nautical miles.

There was more news to come of Chinese infrastructure activities, always a prelude to military presence, from Maldives too.

In December 2016, China was able to get a 50-year lease of a Maldivian island, Feydhoo Finolhu, located three nautical miles from Male, the capital of Maldives. Soon thereafter, a Chinese firm replaced an Indian firm to expand the Velana international airport in Maldives.

Laamu Atoll, the largest atoll in Maldives saw construction activities by Chinese firms for a link-road in form of a gift by China that connected the 12 inhabited islands that comprise this atoll. Chinese firms started developing links with the other industries in Laamu, such as fisheries.

Laamu is of strategic relevance to China as it has a 50-mile-wide and one-and-a-half-degree deep water channel to the south of Laamu, and it is through this deep-water channel through which the east-west sea traffic passes through the archipelago.

Subsequently, Chinese military activity has been noticed in the Laamu Atoll.

In 2023, Mohamed Muizzu, who became the President of Maldives and has a strong pro-China tilt, passed orders for the 75-strong Indian Armed Forces troops stationed in Maldives to leave the island nation by May 10, 2024. He led a successful India-Out election campaign in the run-up to the elections in 2023.

On March 04, 2024, Maldives and China signed a defence cooperation agreement in which China committed to give Maldives free military assistance. Milton Friedman's quote "There's no such thing as a free lunch", needs no explanation in context of this defence deal between China and Maldives.

On March 11, 2024, Maldives purchased the highly sophisticated Bayraktar TB-2 drones from Turkey amidst heightened tensions with India, for reasons of maritime surveillance. However, there is more than what meets the eye.

Maldives has 17 airstrips in its 26 atolls. The North-South extent of these 26 atolls is 820 kilometres and the east-west extent is 130 kilometres. However, all the Bayraktar TB-2 drones have been deployed in only two airstrips of Hoarafushi and Hanimaadhoo, which are a mere 146 kilometres and 176 kilometres respectively from the Minicoy Islands of India. Interestingly, just a few days earlier on March 06, 2024, India had commissioned a new naval base, INS Jatayu, in the Minicoy Islands. The intentions of Maldives thus need no further elaboration.

With Myanmar and Maldives under its tight grasp, China's grip on the String of Pearls is getting stronger.

Alongside development of infrastructure and defence reforms that are quintessential in a country honing up its combat power and combat potential, the strategies for conduct of war too play a very important role when the balloon goes up (a military slang signifying the entry of a nation in war).

The Chinese War Strategy

Modern wars are fought on three levels – strategic, operational and tactical.

Carl von Clausewitz, a Prussian General and a military theorist in his book *"Vom Kriege"* ("On War"), published in 1832 a year after his death by his wife, spoke of two levels of war – strategy and tactical.

It was Aleksandr A. Svechin, an Officer of the Soviet Red Army who in 1920s, first spoke of an operational level of war.

It was much later in 1982, that the US Army adopted all the three levels of war viz. strategic, operational and tactical in their *Field Manual 100-5, Operations*.

The three levels of war all help achieve national objectives. While there are no finite limits or boundaries between these three levels of war, but nature of objective of the mission and the resources employed in achieving the same.

The US Joint Publication (JP 1), *Doctrine for the Armed Forces of the United States* and JP 3-0, *Joint Operations* explain the division between the three levels of war well.

At the strategic level of war is the national policy and the theatre strategy. The operational level of war comprises campaigns and major operations. While the tactical level of war encompasses battles, engagements and small-unit and crew actions.

Modern warfare has traditionally followed the war doctrines enumerated by the US Military as the US Military has been long regarded as a potent and professional fighting force and have been regular in publishing war doctrines, which many nations the world over follow.

Also, since the USA leads North Atlantic Treaty Organisation (NATO), the largest military alliance in the world and the six of the world's ten biggest arms manufacturing firms are located in the USA, the American war doctrines have been considered a good output of experience and inventory of weapons, needed to win wars.

In the subsequent paragraphs, the strategic level of war will be discussed in detail, as it will play a pivotal role in a nation winning a war due to the immense technological advancements the weapon systems have seen in that last about two decades and the new domains of war that have been added.

Till 1982, almost all nations of the world followed the *Active Defence Doctrine* of the US Army which envisioned largely static defence and had the army units moving from one blocking position to the other. This included mobile forces which would be capable of limited offensive in the enemy's territory.

The US Military introduced the *Airland Battle Doctrine* in 1982, which stated close coordination between the Army and the Air Force that would result in formulation of an integrated attack plan, which would entail the land forces in a counter-blitz role while air power, artillery and special forces would stop the movement of the enemy's reserves to the forward lines.

Till today most nations of the world follow the *Airland Battle Doctrine* of 1982, though much has changed since then.

After the success of the Gulf War of 1991, militarily known as *Operation Desert Storm*, which lasted from January 17, 1991 to February 28, 1991, saw the USA led 42-nation coalition, exhibit unprecedented level of professionalism, that included a whopping 1,000 aircraft sorties being undertaken daily, which were totally decided by computers based on the daily inputs given. The USA promulgated the *Full Spectrum Operations Doctrine* in 2001, replacing the *Airland Battle Doctrine* of 1982.

The *Full Spectrum Operations Doctrine* of 2001 enshrined that the cumulative effect of dominance in air, land, maritime, space domains and information environment that includes cyberspace that permits the conduct of joint operations without effective opposition or prohibitive interference. This would espouse a strategic intent capable of achieving full spectrum superiority in a conflict, enabling the control of any situation across the range of military operations, by defeating any adversary.

Surprisingly, China became the only nation in the world to publicly declare its competency and capability to fight any nation in the world in consonance with the *Full Spectrum Operations Doctrine*.

In 2014, PLA in its military doctrine stated that it is ready to fight any country anywhere in the world in all the six domains of war consisting: land, sea, air, cyber, electromagnetic spectrum and space.

Interestingly, such a declaration has not been made till date by any military of the world including the USA, who despite propounding the *Full Spectrum Operations Doctrine* in 2001, lay basking in its success of the 1991 Gulf War, whilst China stealthily and secretly worked towards establishing supremacy in the full spectrum operations warfare, pretty much understanding well how the future modern wars would be fought.

It was precisely in this backdrop that Hu Jintao, China's Paramount Leader in 2004, called upon the PLA to protect China's overseas interests by giving a set of four tasks to the PLA, officially known as the *"Historic Missions of Our Military in the New Century of the New period"* or simply as the *"New Historic Missions"*. The four tasks spelt out by Hu Jintao under this directive were –

- Reinforcing the PLA's loyalty to the CCP
- Ensuring China's continued economic development by defending China's sovereignty, territorial integrity and domestic security
- Defend China's expanding national interests especially in the maritime, space and cyber domains
- Prevent the outbreak of conflict

The first three tasks spelt out by Hu Jintao, were implemented in letter and spirit, leading to the PLA declaring in its 2014 military doctrine that it was ready to fight any nation the world over, in all the six domains of war. Ironically, the last task would turn out to be contrary to the public and perceived opinion and China would be ready to fight six wars in the next 50 years, for which Xi Jinping resorted to the 2015 and 2024 Military Reforms that have been discussed in detail, earlier in this chapter.

The Chinese War Strategy in future wars that it will fight, will be totally on the *Full Spectrum Operations Doctrine.*

An example of the Chinese expertise in multi-domain warfare can be gauged on October 07, 2023, when Hamas launched an attack 15 miles inside Israel at 6:30 am and the Israeli Defence Forces (IDF), one of the most sophisticated and capable defence forces of the world, were caught unaware. This was because from 6.30 a.m. to 6.50 a.m., for a period of twenty minutes, the entire electromagnetic spectrum of the IDF was jammed by Hamas, and thus the IDF did not know for these twenty minutes that over 1000 Hamas personnel had infiltrated 15 miles inside Israel causing mayhem and bloodbath.

Hamas could not have done such a big thing of jamming the electromagnetic spectrum of the IDF on its own as it is a highly specialised field. Definitely there was an external factor which supported Hamas in this daring attack on Israel. Thus, having many nations have a rethink on the military doctrine of the Airland Battle concept of 1982. And the only external factor is China, as it is the solitary world leader in multi-domain warfare.

The wars that China will unleash in the coming years will be different from the *Airland Battle Doctrine* of 1982, as they will first launch cyber-attacks, electromagnetic spectrum and space attacks, before sending their ground forces into their enemy country or launching their air force or naval power. The cyber, electromagnetic spectrum and space attacks will effectively jam the entire networking of the country and they will be without any communication whatsoever, thus throwing all systems in disarray.

In strategic terms, the PLARF and the PLAISF will first cause mayhem and destruction in the other nations' army, navy and the air force and critical civil infrastructure like banking and electricity grids, and then the PLAGF, PLAAF and PLAN will enter the war scenario to achieve the specific strategic aims in a short and swift war.

Six wars that China will fight in the next 50 years

On July 08, 2013, an article was published in Wenweipo, which is pro-China newspaper published from Hong Kong, titled *"Six Wars China is Sure to Fight in the Next 50 Years"*.

The six wars mentioned in the article along with the block dates given for each of these six wars are as follows –

- The 1st War is for Taiwan in 2025–2030

- The 2nd War is for Spratly Islands in 2025–2030

- The 3rd War is a two-front war jointly by Pakistan & China on India in 2035–2040

- The 4th War is for Senkaku Islands in 2040–2045

- The 5th War is for Mongolia in 2045–2050

- The 6th War is for the land lost to Russia in 2055–2060

In this book, the first three wars for Taiwan, Spratly Island and two-front war with India will be discussed and the last three wars will be discussed in the sequel to this book, likely to be published around 2035.

Coming to the first three wars mentioned in the article published in Wenweipo, all timelines and events in the last decade are pointing towards the above-mentioned timeframe.

It is a well-known fact that nothing can be spoken or written in China without the approval of the CCP. So, for an article of this nature with specifics of war and block years being mentioned, does raise hackles and are a matter of immense concern.

This article of Wenweipo was published four months after Xi Jinping was sworn in as the President of China in March 2013. Interestingly, two months after the publication of this article, Xi Jinping announced the BRI in September 2013.

China as a nation has an uncanny quality that whatever it plans decades ahead, its broad plans are always put in public domain, be it in form of press releases or articles published in the totally state-controlled media.

Above all, China's national security strategy termed as *"Comprehensive National Security"* is in public domain. The advantages of having a national security strategy in public domain is that all organisations of the nation work in unison and have a uniformed approach in achieving the national aims and objectives, through any form military or non-military.

The depth and importance of the article of Wenweipo can be gauged by four important events that have occurred in the last couple of years, which clearly show that this article and the timelines can't be ignored, and ignoring it will prove to be fatal and disastrous in the years ahead.

- The US National Security Strategy of 2022, lists China as their primary threat and not their traditional super power rival, Russia, even in the backdrop of the ongoing Russia-Ukraine War.

- On January 27, 2023, General Micheal A. Minihan, the head of the US Air Mobility Command, in an unusual letter to the officers under his command, exhorted them to be ready for a war with China over Taiwan in a few years' time.

- And going a step further, William Burns, the Director of Central Intelligence Agency (CIA), America, officially tasked with gathering, processing and analysing national security information from around the world, said in a statement on February 03, 2023, that the USA and China will go to war over Taiwan in 2027.

- And finally, the US President Joe Biden in his State of the Union address on February 07, 2023, vowed to protect the USA from China, in case China threatened the American sovereignty.

As per a report by the UN Population Division, the population of China in 2100 would be 771 million and of India would be 1,533 million. Hence China knows that whatever it has to do whether with India or Taiwan has to be well before 2100.

Also, the US Intelligence has always been correct on their assessments on future wars. The nations who have ignored American intelligence inputs have done so at the cost of peril to their nations.

The USA had warned Ukraine of an impending Russian attack. Ukraine ignored the inputs and the result is for all to see. It has been more than two years since the Russia-Ukraine War began. The USA warned Israel of a Hamas attack. It has been more than ten months of the ongoing Israel-Hamas War. The USA warned Israel on April 12, 2024, that Iran will attack Israel within 48 hours. On April 14, 2024, Iran attacked Israel with over 200 missiles and drones.

The next war that the USA has warned is China's war for Taiwan in 2027.

Clearly, the war clouds of China have started thickening.

5

The Taiwan War

Taiwan, which is officially known as the Republic of China (ROC), is an independent country located in East Asia at the junction of the East China Sea and the South China Sea, and has 168 islands and with a combined area of 36,193 square kilometres. The main island of Taiwan, which was formerly known as Formosa, has an area of 35,808 square kilometres. Taipei is the capital city of Taiwan and the country has a population of 23.9 million as of April 2023.

The People's Republic of China (PRC) is located on Taiwan's northwest across the 180-kilometre-wide Taiwan Strait, and Japan is in Taiwan's northeast and Philippines onto its south. The eastern part of Taiwan overlooks the wide expanse of the Pacific Ocean, whose control is of paramount importance to both the USA and China.

Taiwan is a sub-tropical island, most of which is covered with rugged mountains that rise to over 13,000 feet in height. These mountains are located on the eastern part of Taiwan facing the Pacific Ocean and are sparsely populated.

Bulk of the Taiwanese population resides in its western part, known as the Western Coastal Plain that faces China. This plain is criss-crossed by east-west rivers, with the most prominent river being Chuo Shuei-Hsi, which is between the Changhua and Yunlin counties.

Taiwan is administratively divided into 22 sub-national divisions comprising six special municipalities, three cities and 13 counties.

Taiwan is not only important to China from the strategic point of view but also from a historical point of view, as China has since long regarded Taiwan as its integral territory and the Chinese administrative maps show Taiwan as China's 23rd Province, despite Taiwan being an independent nation with its own constitution, flag and currency.

Thus, there are two reasons that China wants to annex Taiwan – historical and strategic.

Historic Importance of Taiwan for China

The Qing dynasty of China ruled over Taiwan from 1683 to 1895, after its army led by General Shi Lang defeated the Kingdom of Tungning, also known as Tywan by the British at that time, in the decisive Battle of Penghu in July 1683. Taiwan was formally annexed by China in April 1684.

At that time most Chinese scholars regarded Taiwan as a "speck of dirt on the outer seas with naked, tattooed savages not worthy of spending our resources on". As a twist and turn of times, Taiwan would become priority number one for Chinese annexation four centuries later, apart from being a nationally emotive issue for China.

But General Shi Lang argued that the strategic location of Taiwan was of paramount importance and Taiwan falling in hands of foreign powers would create trouble for the Qing dynasty.

In 1895, the Qing dynasty ceded Taiwan to the Empire of Japan, following the defeat of the Qing dynasty to the Empire of Japan in the First Sino-Japanese War that lasted from July 25, 1894 to April 17, 1895.

Under the Treaty of Shimonoseki, also known as the Treaty of Maguan, China not only ceded Taiwan (then named Formosa), but also lost suzerainty over Korea, besides paying war indemnity to Japan and opening China to Japan for trade.

The Republic of China overthrew the Qing dynasty in 1912 following the 1911 Revolution, also known as the Xinhai Revolution or the Hsinhai Revolution, which ended 2132 years of Imperial rule in China and 276 years of the rule of the Qing dynasty.

In 1945, following the defeat of Japan in World War II, Taiwan once again came under the control of mainland China, then known as the Republic of China, following the issuance of General Order No. 1 by the US General Douglas Mac Arthur on September 02, 1945.

But peace was nowhere in sight in China as the second phase of the civil war in China broke out between the Kuomintang-led government of the Republic of China (then mainland China) and the Chinese Communist Party few days before the end of the World War II, on August 10, 1945 that would eventually end on December 07, 1949, with the defeat of Kuomintang.

This defeat of Kuomintang in the Chinese Civil War led to the Nationalist government of the Republic of China under Chiang Kai-shek retreating to Taiwan, and officially renaming Taiwan as the new Republic of China (ROC).

The CCP after winning the civil war renamed mainland China as the People's Republic of China (PRC).

Thus, two Chinas came into existence, with each of them claiming as the original China or One China, and this would set the platform for prolonged confrontation between PRC and ROC, also known as China and Taiwan, respectively.

China ensured the expulsion of Taiwan from the United Nations (UN), as it threatened to withdraw from the United Nations if it adopted the position of "Two Chinas". It is indeed ironical that though ROC had been one of the founding members of the United Nations, the UN under Resolution 2758 expelled ROC and included PRC in its folds in 1971.

This global blunder that the UN did in 1971 by expelling ROC, which was supported by the USA that time, would cause international upheavals as time would prove in future.

China has been successful in isolating Taiwan internationally, and as a result, Taiwan has diplomatic relations with only 12 nations out of the 193 member nations of the United Nations. China, by way of its economic prowess has loaned money to 166 nations in the world, thus giving it a potent tool to ensure the diplomatic isolation of Taiwan.

The past seven decades have also seen three major conflagrations between China and Taiwan which are called as the First, Second and the Third Taiwan Strait Crisis. While the First and the Second Taiwan Crisis resulted in fatal casualties to both the Chinese and the Taiwanese soldiers, the Third Taiwan Crisis did not have any loss of life. Ironically, all the three Taiwan Strait Crisis ended after intervention of the USA, and the threat to use nuclear weapons on China in order to protect Taiwan.

Taiwan's Strategic Importance for China

Thus, Taiwan's strategic location led to the formulation of the Island Chain Strategy, as the fall of Taiwan to China, will render the Pacific Ocean open to unhindered and unchecked military activities of China, thereby establishing the Chinese hegemony in this ocean.

The Pacific Ocean is the largest and deepest of the Earth's five oceans and is of immense economic and military importance. The Pacific Ocean holds more than 50% of the world's marine and river fish and 89% of the global aquaculture. With eight of the top ten aquaculture producing economies located in this region, the region accounts for 68% of the total world inland fishery production. Also, 60% of the global maritime trade occurs through the waters of the Pacific Ocean.

Militarily, the wide expanse of the Pacific Ocean provides strategic depth to the west coast of the USA, with Taiwan standing as a great natural fortress between eastern China and western USA. The Pacific Ocean is the host to important US allies like Australia and New Zealand, apart from the island nations of Pacific Islands, whom China has been desperate to woo. For, some of these Pacific Island nations have been important military logistical bases during the World War II.

The USA well understood the importance of Taiwan and the criticality of safeguarding both the Indian Ocean and Pacific Ocean Regions, conjointly called as the Indo-Pacific Region. Hence, the Island Chain Strategy was formulated in 1951 by John Foster Dulles, a visionary US foreign affairs expert which enumerated the need to contain the erstwhile USSR and China with a string of naval bases in the western Pacific region to restrict sea access to these two countries.

This strategy did not gain much traction during the Cold War, but after the USSR broke up into 15 countries on December 26, 1991, the Island Chain Strategy gained momentum to contain China, whose growing economic prowess and its desire for hegemony in the Indo-Pacific region was slowly coming out of the closet by now.

The strategy encompasses three island chains- the First Island Chain, the Second Island Chain and the Third Island Chain, all three of which are in the Pacific Ocean.

Of late, it has been proposed to create a Fourth and a Fifth Island Chain too in the Indian Ocean. Thus, the five Island Chains of the Island Chain Strategy would endeavour to checkmate China and contain its dreams for control over the Indo-Pacific region.

The First Island Chain comprises the Kuril Islands, the Japanese Archipelago, Ryuku Islands, Taiwan, northwest Philippines and ending at Borneo. This chain is also the first line of defence and serves as the maritime boundaries between the East China Sea and the Philippine Sea and the South China Sea and the Sulu Sea. In this chain are located the Bashi Channel and the Miyako Strait, which are critical chokepoints for China.

The Second Island Chain consists the Bonin Islands, Volcano Islands, Mariana Islands, eastern Caroline Islands and western New Guinea. This chain is the eastern maritime boundary of the Philippine Sea. The visit of the US Secretary of Defence's visit to the tiny nation of Palau in August 2020, highlights the importance being accorded to this chain. The USA has Compacts of Free Association (COFAs) agreements with Palau, Marshall Islands and Micronesia, all located in this chain, over scoring the interest of the USA in this chain.

The Third Island Chain refers to the Aleutian Islands running through the centre of the Pacific Ocean via the Hawaiian Islands, American Samoa, Fiji, culminating at New Zealand. In this chain New Zealand, Tonga, Hawaii plays an important role. Tonga a small nation with a large Exclusive Economic Zone of 676,401 square kilometres and located 2,330 kilometres from New Zealand and 5,000 kilometres from Hawaii, needs special attention as it a fertile region for Chinese investments and interests.

The Fourth Island Chain proposes to have the Lakshadweep Islands, Maldives, Diego Garcia with Gwadar and Hambantota in Pakistan and Sri Lanka respectively. Though China has managed to take over Gwadar and Hambantota ports, but with the inner turmoil in Pakistan and Sri Lanka due to the Chinese debt trap and other reasons, the USA has its eyes firmly set up on these two ports and is looking for an opportune moment to take them over from the Chinese grip.

The Fifth Island Chain is planned to originate from Camp Lemonnier in the Gulf of Aden, around the Horn of Africa, along the East African coastline, through the Mozambique Channel towards South Africa, with the aim of encircling the Chinese naval bases in Doraleh and Djibouti.

Though the Fourth & Fifth Island Chains are proposals and haven't been put into actualities yet, but with China going aggressively with its BRI and having security pacts with the strategically located Solomon Islands and the Vanatu Islands, the

Fourth & Fifth Island Chains don't seem too far away in being implemented.

Thus, the fall of Taiwan to China will render the collapse of the entire Island Chain Strategy and will throw open the entire Pacific Ocean Region open to the Chinese hegemony.

Initial Turbulence in Taiwan

After the Chinese Civil War ended in 1949, the CCP was sure that sooner than later, Taiwan would implode internally as Taiwan was then financially very poor, and the original inhabitants weren't happy with a large influx of people from the mainland to this small island.

Kuomintang was highly unpopular in Taiwan since Japan had handed over the control of Taiwan to China. On February 28, 1947, the Kuomintang troops carried out a massive slaughter of thousands of Taiwanese that is often compared with the Holocaust carried out by the Germans on Jews. The exact numbers of those killed on this day is unknown but an estimate puts in between 18,000 to 28,000. This massacre on an unprecedented scale is known as the *February 28 Incident* also called as the *February 28 Massacre*.

Thousands more were to die in the subsequent months, as the Kuomintang, sensing certain defeat in mainland China, became more aggressive as the local residents of Taiwan became more resistive to the presence of Kuomintang on their island.

Over two million Chinese nationalists, comprising mainly soldiers, members of Kuomintang and from other walks of life, retreated to Taiwan, adding to six million native residents that resided already in Taiwan. This increased tensions in the island and the Kuomintang declared Martial Law on Taiwan in May 19, 1949, as the defeat of Kuomintang started becoming imminent in mainland China. The Martial Law was in force in Taiwan till July 15, 1987. This period of martial law in Taiwan is known as *White Terror*.

Temporary Provisions Effective During the Period of National Mobilization for Suppression of the Communist Rebellion were the provisions of the *Constitution of the Republic of China*, adopted on December 25, 1947, that effectively nullified the Taiwanese Constitution and established Martial Law in the territories governed by Kuomintang in Taiwan.

The reason given for Martial Law imposition was the ongoing Chinese Civil War, resulting in the curtailment of civil and political freedoms with sweeping powers being vested in the Kuomintang forces.

During this period of Martial Law, any person suspected of either being a Leftist or sympathetic towards the Communists was either arrested or killed. No one was allowed to speak against the Kuomintang government, and those doing so were persecuted, with basic human rights and right to privacy brazenly disregarded.

The Martial Law in Taiwan has the dubious distinction of being the second-longest martial law imposed in any nation, after Syria's 48-year long period of martial law that lasted from 1963 to 2011.

On March 06, 1987, a Vietnamese refugees laden-boat arrived in Kinmen, also known as Quemoy, which is a group of islands governed as a county by Taiwan and is located just 10 kilometres east of Xiamen in the Fujian province of China and 187 kilometres from Taiwan, across the Taiwan Strait.

The Vietnamese refugees in this boat had been rejected by Hong Kong for seeking political asylum, and after their rejection they reached Kinmen to request political asylum. However, their request was denied and this boat was towed away on the morning of March 07, 1987, by an ARB-101 patrol boat with a warning not to return.

This information of the boat's presence was not forwarded to the coastal defence units, including those stationed on Lieyu Island, located to the west of Greater Kinmen and east of Xiamen. In the ensuing circumstances compounded by the onset of seasonal heavy fog in the afternoon, at around 16.37 hours, the boat which by now was stranded on the sand beach southwest of Donggang, was hit by armour-piercing shells fired by the Kinmen Defence Command, which resulted in substantial damage to the boat. All 19 survivors of the boat were shot dead, subsequently, their bodies were buried.

The incident of March 07, 1987, known as the *1987 Lieyu Massacre* or the *March 7 Incident* created a huge furore internationally, leading to the US House of Representatives passing the *Taiwan Democracy Resolution* on June 17, 1987, which finally resulted in the end of Martial Law in Taiwan a month later.

Taiwan than transited to democracy, which also saw the nation undergoing a process of localisation and Taiwanese culture and history being promoted over a pan-China viewpoint and assimilationist policies being replaced by multiculturalism.

Hence, Taiwan did not implode internally as the CCP had expected it to happen soon after the end of the Chinese Civil War. Rather, Taiwan rose economically like a phoenix despite these internal turbulences, due to certain economic reforms and measures, known as the *Taiwan Miracle*.

The Taiwan Miracle

As the Kuomintang government started firming its control over Taiwan after fleeing from mainland China towards the end of the Chinese Civil War, apart from the internal upheaval in Taiwan, it was also besieged with the problems of hyperinflation and its agricultural economy in shambles.

Chiang Kai-shek was clear on landing in Taiwan, as the defeat of the Nationalist government became imminent in the Chinese Civil War, that in case Taiwan was to resist the take-over by the CCP, economic growth would be of paramount importance, notwithstanding the internal disturbances.

The USA came to the rescue of Taiwan, during its initial stages as a young nation by giving US$ 4 billion in financial aid and soft credit during the period 1945–1965. Thus, with the initial capital now available, the Kuomintang government instituted land reforms and enacted new laws to transition Taiwan to a better economic future.

Under the land reforms three majors programme were instituted: selling public land to tenant farmers, limiting the rent to 37.5% of the expected harvest, and restricting the size of individual landholdings. These land reforms resulted in creation of a large number of peasants that eventually increased the agricultural output dramatically.

While focusing on the agrarian sector, the Kuomintang government quite well understood the importance of industrialisation. Quick industrialisation started paying rich dividends and soon Taiwan came to known globally for its cheap manufactured exports produced by small enterprises interwoven together by flexible sub-contracting networks.

In the 1950s, Taiwan underwent through a period of importing substitution policy, in which the domestic manufacturers were benefited by tariffs and multiple overvalued exchange rates. The period of 1960s and 1970s saw the promotion of manufactured exports that included the setting up of export processing zones.

This dual focus on the agrarian sector and industrialisation started paying rich dividends and during the period 1960 to 1980, the GDP grew 10% each year with the per capita GDP increasing 7% annually.

This also resulted in the Taiwanese dollar stabilising and the saving rates increasing. Education enrolment increased manifold, both at the school and higher education level.

The social gap between the rich and the poor reduced drastically from the score on Gini falling from 0.558 in 1953 to 0.303 in 1980. Infrastructure, healthcare and quality of life improved significantly.

After Taiwan was expelled by the United Nations, it was quick to realize that leadership in manufacturing niche products would be essential to avoid international isolation that was staring on it now.

The Kuomintang government started a process of enhancement and modernisation of industry and several technology parks were constructed with a new-found focus on manufacturing microelectronics, personal computers and peripherals.

The 1980s saw Taiwan's rise as a major economic power, and apart from a reckonable presence in international markets, Taiwan not only started investing abroad but now had sizeable foreign exchange reserves too.

This remarkable economic rise earned Taiwan a place in the list of *Four Asian Tigers*, alongside Hong Kong, Singapore and South Korea, as these four economies had developed into high-income economies, and they soon became role models for many developing countries.

The magnificent economic rise of Taiwan can be seen by just one economic statistics. In 1952, Taiwan has a per capita Gross National Product of US$ 170 which soared to US$ 53,074 in 2018.

Previous Military Attempts for Annexation of Taiwan

As Taiwan started rising economically, it became clear to the CCP that neither would Taiwan implode internally nor would it cede back to China. Hence, the only option left for China to take over Taiwan was militarily.

Added to the growing despair in China was that not only was Taiwan increasing its economic power, it was overtaking China in economic prosperity due to the land reforms launched by Chiang Kai-shek. This was upsetting China and it was shameful that a breakaway country was galloping its way up the economic ladder.

Though in 1949, China was better than Taiwan economically but things started changing soon thereafter. China could well foresee that the land reforms being instituted by Taiwan would bear fruit, as apart from the fact that they were aware of Chiang Kai-shek's functioning, similar land reforms in Japan had yielded positive results. The despair in the CCP was increasing with each passing day to annex Taiwan.

Three major military attempts have since been undertaken by China to annex Taiwan, but each of them was unsuccessful as the USA always stood rock-solid behind Taiwan. These military attempts are called the *Taiwan Strait Crisis*.

The first military attempt for the Taiwanese takeover by China did not have to wait for too long after the CCP victory in the Chinese Civil war that ended in 1949. The *First Taiwan Strait Crisis* also known as the *Formosa Crisis*, lasted from September 03, 1954 to May 01, 1955, saw 519 Taiwanese and two Americans killed while 393 Chinese lost their lives. The main focus of this military operation by China was to occupy the several group of Taiwanese islands that were located just a few nautical miles from mainland China, the prominent ones being Kinmen, Matsu and Tachen.

On August 11, 1954, Zhou Enlai, the Chinese Premier declared that Taiwan must be liberated. The PLA was mobilised, and shelling of Kinmen started on September 03, 1954, which resulted in two US military advisers being killed the same day. Soon thereafter, shelling of Tachen started.

On December 02, 1954, the USA and Taiwan signed the *Sino-American Mutual Defense Treaty*, with the sole intention of defending Taiwan from an invasion by China. This treaty lasted from 1955–1980, and was subsequently replaced by the Taiwan Relations Act 1979, enacted by the United States Congress.

As the *First Taiwan Crisis* raged on, China seized the Yijiangshan Islands on January 18, 1955, and combat started in the nearby islands too. On January 29, 1955, the *Formosa Resolution* was approved by both the houses of the US Congress, which authorised the US President to defend Taiwan and its islands in the Taiwan Strait against any invasion.

US Navy started assisting the Taiwanese forces against the Chinese invasion. In March 1955, the US Secretary of State, John Foster Dallas, stated that US was considering a nuclear strike on China. This had a serious effect on China, and in April 1955, Zhou Enlai stated that China did not want to go to war with the USA, which eventually resulted in the de-escalation of the *First Taiwan Strait Crisis*.

Two things made China end its invasion. One, the world was fresh with the atomic disasters unleashed by the USA in Hiroshima and Nagasaki just a few years back in 1945. Two, and the most important, China had no nuclear capability.

Thus ended the *First Taiwan Strait Crisis* on May 01, 1955, with a total fatal casualty of 914 personnel.

The *Second Taiwan Strait Crisis* also known as the *1958 Taiwan Strait Crisis*, occurred a few years later from August 23 to December 02, 1958, which resulted in 594 Taiwanese dying and 460 Chinese being killed.

On August 23, 1958, the PLA began shelling of Kinmen and some of the nearby Matsu islands, controlled by the Republic of China Armed Forces, also known as the ROC Armed Forces. The next two days saw heavy fighting between the two adversaries when the PLA attempted an amphibious landing on the Dongding Island of Taiwan.

As the war raged between China and Taiwan, on September 02, 1958, the US Secretary of State, John Foster Dulles met with the Joint Chiefs of Staff, which is the body of the senior uniformed Officers of the United States Department of Defence that advises the US President on military matters. It was decided in the meeting that though initially US would use conventional forces in this war to assist Taiwan, but if the need arises, then nuclear weapons would be used too.

The USA deployed its famed US Navy Seventh Fleet in the region, apart from scrambling fighter aircrafts like F-100D Super Sabres and F-101C Voodoos to demonstrate its combat support to Taiwan.

Also, the US Navy started escorting Taiwanese Navy ships from Taiwan to Kinmen and back. China stopped its artillery shelling whenever it observed US Navy warships escorting the warships of the Taiwanese Navy.

Underway at that time was a secret operation codenamed *Operation Black Magic*, in which the US Navy secretly modified the F-86 Sabre fighter aircrafts of the Taiwanese Air Force to be capable of deploying the newly developed AIM-9 Sidewinder air-to-air missiles. This strategic move gave the Taiwanese Air Force a decisive edge over the PLAAF's Soviet-made MiG-15 and MiG-17 fighter aircrafts during the *Second Taiwan Strait Crisis*.

On October 06, 1958, China announced a unilateral ceasefire as the PLA Artillery had finished all its artillery shells. But after a few days, resumed the artillery shelling on October 20, 1958 due to two reasons. One, a US Navy warship breached the China-declared three nautical miles exclusive zone from the China coast. Two, the US Secretary of State, John Foster Dulles arrived in Taipei to take stock of the ongoing war.

The *Second Taiwan Strait Crisis* officially ended on December 02, 1958, with both China and Taiwan declaring victory. In actual, China had lost yet another war to annex Taiwan, as the USA stood firmly behind Taiwan and China still hadn't any nuclear weapons.

The next military attempt by China to annex Taiwan would come after more than three decades in the form of *The Third Taiwan Strait Crisis* also known as the *1996 Taiwan Strait Crisis*.

The Third Taiwan Strait Crisis began in a rather unmilitary background when President Lee Teng-hui, the President of Taiwan during whose currency as the Taiwanese President, the martial law ended and Taiwan became a democracy, decided to accept an invitation in 1995 from his alma mater, the Cornell

University in Ithaca, New York, USA, to deliver a speech on "Taiwan's Democratisation Experience".

China vehemently opposed the USA giving a visa to President Lee Teng-hui as by that time the USA in accordance with the *One China* principle was diplomatically recognising China and not Taiwan.

However, the US Congress passed a concurrent resolution, allowing the issuance of visa to President Lee Teng-hui and the Taiwanese President visited the USA on June 09–10, 1995, to deliver the speech. China was infuriated and branded the Taiwanese president as a traitor attempting to "split China".

Jiang Zemin, the Third Paramount Leader of China, extremely furious and angry over the Taiwanese President's visit to the USA, ordered the mobilisation of PLA and directed PLA to conduct missiles tests on July 07, 1995. The missile tests began on July 21, 1995 and lasted a few days with the sole aim of intimidating Taiwan.

Live ammunition military exercises were conducted by China from August 15–25, 1995, followed by naval amphibious assault exercises. The USA immediately responded to China's military overtures by sending two aircraft carrier groups in the vicinity of Taiwan – the USS McClusky and the USS Nimitz in December 1995.

On March 08, 1996, US President Bill Clinton announced that the Carrier Strike Group 5, would deploy in international waters near Taiwan. However, undeterred by all these American naval deployments, China continued its live ammunition firing exercises.

On March 11, 1996, the USA despatched its Carrier Strike Group 7 from the Persian Gulf to the international waters near Taiwan.

With two US Navy Carrier Strike Groups stationed near Taiwan, China had no option and the *Third Taiwan Strait Crisis* ended on March 23, 1996, in a whimper with no combat taking place between China and Taiwan.

Thus, the *Third Taiwan Strait Crisis* lasted from July 21, 1995 till March 23, 1996, but fortunately there were no casualties on either side.

China then realised that such attempts to annex Taiwan would be futile as the USA stood firmly behind Taiwan and the only way that Taiwan could be annexed was when China would overtake the USA militarily, but before that China had to become strong economically.

And ironically, it was the USA which was aiding China's rise economically as year-on-year trade between the USA and China was increasing, and each dollar that China was earning out its trade with the USA or any other nation, the PLA was being strengthened in this process.

Lessons Learnt by China after the Three Failed Attempts to Annex Taiwan

With neither Taiwan imploding nor it ceding to China on its own, and to top up the woes of China, were the three failed military attempts to annex Taiwan known as the *Taiwan Strait Crisis*. Jiang Zemin, the third Paramount Leader of China, realised that China could only annex Taiwan if it had a military that was superior to the US military, as the one important factor that resulted in the failure of the *Taiwan Strait Crisis* was the USA's immense military power.

To upgrade the PLA to a world-class military power capable of facing up the challenges being posed by the US military in annexing Taiwan, Jiang Zemin, soon after the end of the *Third Taiwan Strait Crisis*, launched the ten-year military modernisation programme for the PLA.

The four major transitions that China did post-failure of the *Taiwan Strait Crisis* are enumerated below -

- Nuclear Weapons: One of the major lessons that China learnt after the *First Taiwan Strait Crisis* and the *Second Taiwan Strait*

Crisis was that it had no nuclear weapons. Since both the military attempts to annex Taiwan had failed as the USA had openly threatened to use nuclear weapons on China, it was imperative to have a nuclear weapons arsenal.

With the Soviet assistance, China conducted its first nuclear test in Lop Nur on October 16, 1964. In the next 32 years, until 1996, China conducted 45 nuclear tests until it signed the Comprehensive Nuclear Test-Ban Treaty (CTBT). By 1996, China had 234 nuclear weapons. The rise of China as a nuclear power has been discussed in detail in the previous chapter.

- Robust Military Industrial Complex: An important lesson learnt after the failure of the *Second Taiwan Strait Crisis* when China ran out of artillery shells was a robust domestic Military Industrial Complex, similar to what the USA had so that it did not face such a situation in future where lack of weapon systems and ammunition would put China at a disadvantage again. With China rising economically and becoming a global manufacturing hub, attention was also paid to develop the domestic arms industries.

A nation can only have a robust Military Industrial Complex if adequate attention and amount is allocated to Research & Development (R&D) and there are large number of Doctorates in the field of Science, Technology, Engineering & Mathematics (STEM) as these four disciplines play a pivotal role in development of R&D.

In the early 1990s, the nascent Chinese Defence Industry was plagued by inefficiency, poor performance and corruption. For the period 2000–2011, the Chinese defence budget had an upsurge of 11.8% annually and nearly one-third of the annual defence budget was earmarked for R&D. Over 1,000 enterprises sprung up to spearhead China's Military Industrial Complex, employing around 3 million workers.

Jiang Zemin also ensured strategic defence reforms, enabling the private sector to enter defence manufacturing, which till now was the monopoly of Chinese government-controlled firms.

The results were quick to be seen. In 2009, the US Department of Defence in a study observed that China had done well in defence production sectors that were now deeply embedded in the global R&D chain. The study further went to highlight that China had done notably well in aviation, missiles and shipbuilding.

Though many allegations surfaced too, with the USA accusing China of stealing Intellectual Property Rights (IPR) and indulging in reverse-engineering by copying weapon systems and technology from the US Military Industrial Complex by using state-sponsored industrial and economic espionage. But as always, no punitive action was taken on China by any world body and China's Military Industrial Complex continued to soar higher.

China also improved its performance in the Information Technology (IT) sector, and the PLA was quick to leverage IT products and improve the military's command, control, communications, computers and intelligence (C4I) capabilities.

All the above advancements in the capacities and capabilities of China's Military Industrial Complex would play a pivotal role in two important turn of events. One, the PLA declaring in its military doctrine of 2014 that it was capable of fighting any nation in the world in all the six domains of war comprising land, sea, air, cyberspace, electromagnetic spectrum and space. And two, Xi Jinping carrying out the 2015 and 2024 Military Reforms which saw the emergence of PLARF and PLASSF, now known as PLAISF. Both these issues have been discussed in detail in the previous chapter.

- A Strong Navy: After the debacle in the three *Taiwan Strait Crisis*, China realised that its Achilles Heel in the failed military operations to annex Taiwan was its weak Navy as compared to the superior naval force that the Americans enjoyed. Since

Taiwan being an island that lay across a water body called the Taiwan Strait, it was but essential that unless the PLAN was strengthened, capture of Taiwan would be impossible.

In 1996, PLAN had just 57 warships as compared to the 108 warships that the US Navy possessed. Clearly, these numbers would prove vastly inadequate for an assault amphibious takeover of Taiwan. As brought out earlier, that in 2000 the famous joke in the corridors of Pentagon was that for China to reach Taiwan, the PLA would have to swim across the Taiwan Strait!

But things were to change, and the change was to happen soon. Under Jiang Zemin's *Ten-Year Military Modernisation* initiated after China's defeat in the *Third Taiwan Strait Crisis*, focus was also paid to develop a strong maritime force which would be both modern and capable. By 2015, China had pipped the USA in having the world's largest navy as the PLAN had 294 warships and submarines as compared to 289 warships and submarines in the US Navy's inventory. The rise in the capacity and capability of China's shipbuilding power has been discussed at length in the previous chapter.

- Adoption of Full Spectrum Superiority Doctrine: PLA was the first military in the world to realise and adopt that modern wars would no longer be fought in the conventional manner, with a nation's army playing a pivotal role and the air force and navy being deployed for strategic and tactical gains in furtherance of achieving a nation's national objectives and war aims.

  The future wars, as correctly assessed by PLA after the success of the US-led coalition forces in *Operation Desert Storm* in the 1991 Gulf War, would be multi-domain and would follow the principles of full spectrum warfare, a war without any realms or boundaries.

  After Pentagon published the *Full Spectrum Operations Doctrine* in 2001 superseding the *Airland Battle Doctrine* of 1982, PLA became the first and the only nation till date to declare in its military doctrine in 2014, that it was capable in fighting any nation of the world in all six domains of war. This aspect too has been dwelt in detail in the previous chapter.

Thus, the PLA is prepared to fight it next war to annex Taiwan in 2027, and this time the odds of winning the war are loaded heavily in favour of China.

China's 2027 War to Annex Taiwan

When Xi Jinping became the 5th Paramount Leader of China on March 14, 2013, he was clear that with a strong economy, a combat-prepared armed forces, and an ever-increasing nuclear arsenal, the circumstances would be ripe to launch an invasion of Taiwan. This strong economy-military-nuclear combination would ensure military success and eventually the long-cherished dream of every Chinese—the annexation of Taiwan.

But what was to be decided was the timing of the *Fourth Taiwan Strait Crisis*, as the next Chinese war for Taiwan will in all probability be known as, and Sun Tzu's quote *"He will win who knows when to fight and when not to fight"*, would surely have impacted the timing of China's next war for Taiwan.

Probably never in history before has any war been planned for years or decades in advance. Wars are generally planned a year or two in advance when the political leadership of a nation has no option than to use war as its ultimate weapon, when dialogue and diplomacy fail like the 1971 India-Pakistan War. Or, wars happen suddenly due to an incident triggering the outbreak, as in case of the Israel-Hamas War that broke out on October 07, 2023, after Hamas launched an attack inside Israel that took Israel completely by surprise.

But in case of the next China's war for Taiwan, Xi Jinping had at least a decade earlier on becoming the Paramount Leader of China on March 14, 2013, decided that China's next war for Taiwan would be in 2027. For it is in 2027 that the PLA will complete 100 years of its founding, and there could be no better way to celebrate the centennial anniversary of the PLA than to annex Taiwan, which is not only China's foremost national objective but is a national obsession too for every Chinese.

Thus, there can be no better year for China in general and for Xi Jinping, to choose 2027 to annex Taiwan as it would attach immense symbolism and significance in case China is able to annex in 2027.

On March 21, 2024, Admiral John Aquilino, the Commander of the US Indo-Pacific Command, testified to the US House Armed Services Committee that China was on track to be ready for the invasion of Taiwan in 2027. The Admiral further added that China has increased its defence budget by over 16% in recent years to more than US$ 223 billion. Further, he went on to say that in the three years of him assuming command, the PLA has added more than 400 fighter aircrafts and 20 major warships.

Just a year earlier on February 03, 2023, William Burns, the Director of Central Intelligence Agency (CIA), the USA officially tasked with gathering, processing and analysing national security information from around the world, said in a statement that the USA and China will go to war over Taiwan in 2027.

And, on April 21, 2023, Joseph Wu, Taiwan's Foreign Minister in a television interview stated 2027 is the year when China will attack Taiwan and that Taiwan is taking the Chinese military threat very seriously.

Hence it is very clearly evident that China's invasion of Taiwan will happen in 2027, which the following timelines and turn of events are alarmingly pointing to.

- **Modernisation of PLA**: The modernisation of PLA that began with Xi Jinping's 2015 and 2024 Military Reforms is to be completed by 2027. This includes various military exercises being carried out by the newly created five Theatre Commands of the PLA in the run-up to 2027, as only a short and swift military operation will result in the annexation of Taiwan. This is one of the key lessons that China has learnt from the prolonged Russia-Ukraine War that before the USA can rush to Taiwan's aid in case of a military offensive being launched by China, the major portion of China's offensive campaign should be over with the PLA troops well-entrenched in key Taiwanese locations.

The modernisation of PLA includes the large-scale construction of the naval warships and submarines and enhancing the inventory of nuclear weapons, both of which have been discussed in detail in the previous chapter.

- **PLA Military Exercises within ADIZ**: Since 2013, when Xi Jinping became the Paramount Leader of China, the activities of PLA military activities across the Taiwan Strait have increased year-on-year, reaching a crescendo during the period August 04–07, 2022, when the US Speaker Nancy Pelosi visited Taiwan on August 05, 2022. This military exercise was the closest to Taiwan than any previous ones, and were conducted in seven exercise zones by the PLA within Taiwan's Air Defence Identification Zone (ADIZ), encircling Taiwan from all directions. Thus, giving the clearest picture ever how the Chinese invasion of Taiwan would happen.

Wars many times in the past have been started in the garb of military exercises as it is routine for neighbouring adversaries to have regular military exercises. A recent example is the Russia-Ukraine War that started on February 24, 2022, happened in the garb of military exercises that Russia was purportedly carrying on its borders with Ukraine and on the Belarus-Ukrainian border.

Before Xi Jinping became China's Paramount Leader in 2013, rarely did the PLA cross the *Median Line* in the Taiwan Strait, the 180-kilometers water body that separates China and Taiwan. The *Median Line* also known as the *Davis Line* is an imaginary line drawn in the middle of the Taiwan Strait by the

US Air Force General Benjamin O. Davis Jr. in 1955, which though has no official and legal status, but for long was respected by both China and Taiwan. Since, Xi Jinping became China's Paramount Leader in 2013 China has paid scant regard to the *Median Line*.

- **Justification of Xi Jinping's Constitutional Amendment for Presidency:** The 19th National Congress of the CCP in October 2017 discussed and finally unanimously adopted a crucial amendment to the Chinese Constitution, which was the inclusion of *Xi Jinping Thought on Socialism with Chinese Characteristics for a New Era*. In March 2018, the *Xi Thought* as it is also known as, was formally incorporated in the Chinese Constitution, bringing Xi Jinping at the same power pedestal as that of Mao Zedong. Not since Mao Zedong has any Chinese Paramount Leader's ideology been embedded in the Chinese Constitution while still in office. The *Deng Xiaoping Theory* was included in the Chinese Constitution after Deng Xiaoping had passed away.

Xi Thought which comprises eight fundamental issues and 14 fundamental principles, all clearly spell out a "CPC-First" approach.

On December 04, 1982, during the 5th National Congress of the CCP, the new Constitution of China was adopted which had one major feature: no Chinese citizen could become the President of China for more than two terms. This was necessitated to prevent a Mao Zedong-type situation happening where limitless tenures as the President of China had brought mayhem in China in form of either the *Great Leap Forward* or the *Cultural Revolution*, both of which have been discussed in detail in Chapter 2 of this book.

On March 11, 2018, the National Congress of the CCP revoked the two-term limit for the Chinese Presidency, with almost all of the 2,964 delegates voting in favour of this resolution with just two voting against this motion and three abstaining. Thus, effectively paving way for unlimited tenures as China's President for Xi Jinping.

These two major constitutional amendments in the Chinese Constitution, including *Xi's Thought* and having unlimited tenures as China's President have put an immense burden on Xi Jinping's legacy and label. Xi Jinping has to do something that no other Chinese Paramount Leader has ever done earlier, to justify these two path-breaking constitutional amendments.

And what better justification can be to the two constitutional amendments of the Chinese Constitution that have made Xi Jinping a President-for-life and his ideology embedded in the Chinese Constitution, than to annex Taiwan, which is the first and foremost issue on any Chinese citizen's mind.

Apart from the swearing in as the President of China for the third time on March 10, 2023, and the huge responsibility on Xi Jinping of the two major constitutional amendments, it is the age factor that is weighing heavily on Xi Jinping mind.

Born on June 15, 1953, Xi Jinping is 71 years old. The life expectancy of a Chinese male is 78 years. Going by these parameters, Xi Jinping is well aware that he has a few years more at the helm of affairs to do something that China will always remember him and would make his name immortal, and that is to annex Taiwan.

By these parameters, 2027 seems to be the year when China will invade Taiwan as for a few more years after 2027, Xi Jinping will be able to consolidate his win and iron out any international backlash that will follow the Chinese invasion of Taiwan, apart from launching two more wars which will be discussed in the subsequent chapters.

- **National Congress of 2027** – The next National Congress of the CCP is slated in March 2028. At that time Xi Jinping will be under moral obligation and responsibility to tell the National Congress, the justification for the two path-breaking constitutional amendments that were carried out to the

Chinese Constitution in 2018. It will be also the time that Xi Jinping will be seeking the fourth term as China's President. Only annexation of Taiwan will justify Xi Jinping's accession as the Chinese President for a fourth consecutive term.

Aiding and abetting China's military designs for annexation of Taiwan in 2027 is the USA's failure to send soldiers to Ukraine's aid in the prolonged Russia-Ukraine War and to Israel's aid in the ongoing Israel-Hamas War. Clearly, not many allies of the USA trust them to help militarily if the need arises, except for monetary and weapons assistance.

In an article published in *The Guardian* on November 23, 2023, the results of a survey conducted in Taiwan showed that only 34% of the Taiwanese citizens believed that the USA was a stable partner for Taiwan. Also, the survey brought out that 82.7% of the Taiwanese citizens believed that the threat from China has worsened in recent years.

The majority of the Taiwanese aren't wrong in assessing that the USA will not send its soldiers to aid Taiwan, in case of a war with China. In the last decade, the USA has stopped sending its soldiers to aid and assist its allies and friends, when a war besieges them.

Whether its Ukraine in its war with Russia, or Israel with its war with Hamas, or when Iran attacked Israel on April 14, 2024, the USA has not sent any soldier to either Ukraine or Israel.

China is clearly on its well-planned path to annex Taiwan in 2027, and there is nothing that can stop China is this military overture, which would be the next big war on the world's horizon after the 2022 Russia-Ukraine War and the 2023 Israel-Hamas War.

If China is able to annex Taiwan which in all probability it will considering the various factors discussed in this chapter and the previous one, not so later thereafter, will it militarily strike next for Spratly Islands.

6

War for Spratly Islands

In case China is successful in annexing Taiwan in 2027, although it is unlikely that the USA will come to the aid of Taiwan by way of sending soldiers on Taiwanese soil, it is certain that the US military will begin a big show of strength in the international waters surrounding Taiwan.

Importance of the South China Sea

Amongst the international waters surrounding Taiwan is the South China Sea (SCS), which is a huge water body in the Western Pacific Ocean, which encompasses an area of around 3.5 million square kilometres and is located in an important geostrategic location bounded by southern China in its north, Taiwan and northwestern Philippines in the east, and the Indonesian islands of Borneo, eastern Sumatra and the Bangka Belitung Islands in the south, and the Indochinese peninsula in the west.

Also, the South China Sea links with the East China Sea via the Taiwan Strait, the Java Sea by the Karimata and Bangka Straits, the Philippine Sea by the Luzon Strait, and the Sulu Sea by the straits around Palawan. South China Sea also includes the Gulf of Tonkin and the Gulf of Thailand.

Thus, needless to say with such an important geostrategic location, the South China Sea also has an immense geoeconomic significance. The SCS has been an historically important trade route between China, Southeast Asia, India and further up to Western Europe. Of the total world trade that took place in 2023, which was worth US$ 24.90 trillion, more than 22% of it passed through the South China Sea. One-third of the global shipping takes place through the SCS annually.

Ten major countries are majorly dependent on the SCS for their trade, as it is their main lifeline for fuel and other essential commodities. 65% of the total trade of China and 42% of the total trade of Japan passes through the SCS.

Added to the geostrategic and geoeconomic importance of the SCS are the huge untapped petroleum and natural gas reserves that exist in the SCS. It is estimated that 11 billion barrels of oil and 190 trillion cubic feet of natural gas lies untapped in the international waters of the SCS.

The basin countries of the South China Sea are China, Taiwan, Brunei, Vietnam, the Philippines, Malaysia and Indonesia. And thus, between these seven countries, remain disputes and competing claims of sovereignty for the control of SCS.

It was but natural that sooner or later, China would stake claim to the South China Sea given its vast importance. According to ancient Chinese literature, China consisted of *Four Seas*, one for each of the four cardinal directions. The *Four Seas* comprised the West Sea which is the present-day Qinghai Lake, the East Sea which is East China Sea, the North Sea which is currently known as Lake Baikal, and the South Sea which is the most famous of the *Four Seas* and is well-known in the modern era as the South China Sea.

China has a known history of staking claims to internationally recognised boundaries by raking up the past based on ancient literature. And in this case too, nothing different was expected from China from the established past practices.

The International Hydrographic Organisation (IHO) in its *Limits of Oceans and Seas*, 3rd Edition, 1953, has defined the limits of South China Sea very clearly giving out the exact points in the four cardinal directions. In a revised edition of the above report issued vide the 4th Edition in 1986, the southern limit of the SCS was revised from the Bangka Belitung Islands to the Natuna Islands.

Both China and Taiwan claim almost the entire SCS as their own, with China being the most vocal and vociferous in staking claim for SCS by *Nine-Dash Line* and Taiwan stakes claim on the SCS by the *Eleven-Dash Line*, which are a set of line segments on various maps that both these nations base their claim on SCS.

The SCS has over 250 islands, cays, reefs, shoals, sandbars and atolls, of which very few are inhabited. The hotly contested area of the SCS includes: Paracel Islands, the Spratly Islands, the Pratas Islands, the Vereker Banks, the Macclesfield Bank, and the Scarborough Shoal.

On August 28, 2023, China issued a new *Ten-Dash Line* that further raised tempers in the cool and choppy waters of the SCS and the littoral nations that stake claim on the SCS, as well as the international community, for the geostrategic and the geoeconomic importance that SCS holds globally.

While both China and Taiwan claim the SCS based on their *Ten-Dash Line* and *Eleven-Dash Line* theories, there are other claimants for various parts of the SCS.

The waters northeast of the Natuna Islands which is a 154 islands-regency of Indonesia, are claimed by China, Taiwan, Vietnam and Indonesia. China, Taiwan and the Philippines claim the Scarborough Shoal.

China, Taiwan and Vietnam also stake claims to the waters, west of the Spratly Islands. These three countries are also in a dispute over Paracel Islands.

While Thailand, Malaysia, Vietnam and Cambodia have locked horns over areas in the Gulf of Thailand, Singapore and Malaysia have issues over the Strait of Johore and the Strait of Singapore.

South China Sea has seen territorial disputes turn ugly, with blood spilling in its waters and lives being lost in bloody conflicts and battles.

On January 19, 1974, the navies of China and South Vietnam, in the Battle of Paracel Islands, engaged militarily in which 18 Chinese soldiers and 75 South Vietnamese soldiers died, which resulted in the victory of China. Full control of the Paracel Islands was regained by China after this battle. Prior to this battle, both China and South Vietnam controlled parts of the Paracel Islands.

March 1988 saw a bloody clash between Vietnam and China in the Spratly Islands, which resulted in 70 Vietnamese soldiers being killed south of the Chigua Reef, and this time too, China emerged victorious and has since then occupied the Chigua Reef, also known as Johnson South Reef.

In 2014, China started reclamation work in the Chigua Reef, expanding the usable surface area to 10.9 hectares, and building a military base with radars and a small harbour. In 2016, anti-aircraft guns and a Close-in Weapon missile-defence system were deployed on this reef.

The Association of Southeast Asian Nations (ASEAN), a ten-nation alliance comprising Brunei, Cambodia, Indonesia, Laos, Malaysia, Myanmar, the Philippines, Singapore, Thailand and Vietnam, most of which are littoral nations of the SCS and are involved/affected by the various disputes, has been trying since its inception on August 08, 1967, to not let the disputes of SCS escalate into armed conflicts.

In 2008, the International Court of Justice resolved the long-standing dispute of Pedra Blanca and Middle Rocks between Singapore and Malaysia by awarding Pedra Blanca to Singapore and the Middle Rocks to Malaysia.

As the tensions and turbulence in the South China Sea grew, the US Secretary of State Hillary Clinton called upon China in July 2010 to resolve the disputes in the SCS amicably. China responded curtly by telling the USA to remain out of the SCS disputes. This statement and a counter-retort came at a time, when both the US Navy and PLAN were holding maritime exercises in the SCS in a show of strength.

On August 18, 2010, the US Department of Defence, in a statement accused China of assertive behaviour and opposed the use of force to resolve the SCS disputes.

In 2012 and 2013, Vietnam strongly protested at Taiwan carrying out live-fire exercises in the vicinity of Spratly Islands. The next year in May 2014, China established an oil rig near Paracel Islands, leading to an increase in confrontation between China and Vietnam.

On January 22, 2013, the Philippines instituted arbitral proceedings against China under Annex VII to the *United Nations Convention on the Law of the Sea* (UNCLOS). This arbitration sought to encompass the role of historic rights and the source of maritime entitlements in the South China Sea, and the lawfulness of certain actions by China in the SCS that the Philippines were alleged to be in violation of the Convention.

On February 19, 2013, China publicly declared its decision to not participate in the arbitration initiated by the Philippines in UNCLOS.

The UNCLOS was adopted in 1982 and lays down a comprehensive regime of law and order in the world's oceans and seas, establishing rules governing all uses of the maritime waters and their resources. While embodying traditional rules for the uses of oceans and seas, it also introduced new legal concepts and regimes addressing new concerns. UNCLOS also provides the framework for further development of specific areas of the law of the sea.

Part II, Section 3, Subsection A, Articles 17-19 of UNCLOS clearly states that all ships have the right to conduct innocent passage (unarmed, no loading of goods or people etc) on all territorial sea beds. Clearly implying that all ships can traverse within 12 nautical miles from a country's coast, as long as they are not a threat to that nation's security.

However, Part II, Section 3, Subsection A, Articles 22-23 of UNCLOS states that tankers or ships carrying hazardous material may be directed to use specialised sea lanes to conduct their passage through a country's territorial waters.

168 nations are signatory to UNCLOS, including China, who became a signatory to the UNCLOS in 1982 and ratified it in 1996.

On July 12, 2016, UNCLOS announced its decision in the arbitration case initiated by the Philippines, and in a 501-page detailed order ruled that China' historic rights claim over the maritime areas included in the *Nine-Dash Line* have no lawful effect if they exceed what is entitled to under UNCLOS. It further stated that China had no legal basis to claim historic rights to resources with the sea areas falling under the *Nine-Dash Line*.

UNCLOS, in its arbitration ruling, further clarified that under the existing provisions, a group of islands such as the Spratly Islands can't generate maritime zones collectively as a unit. It was unequivocal in adding that China had breached its obligations under the convention on the *International Regulations for Preventing Collisions at Sea* and Article 94 of UNCLOS concerning maritime safety.

As expected, China rejected the arbitration ruling. And interestingly, Taiwan too rejected this arbitration ruling.

During the 36th ASEAN Summit held virtually due to the Covid-19 pandemic on June 26, 2020, Vietnam being the Chairman of ASEAN said in a statement that the UNCLOS is "the basis for determining maritime entitlements, sovereign rights, jurisdiction and legitimate interests over maritime zones, and the 1982 UNCLOS sets out the legal framework within which all the activities in the ocean and seas must be carried out".

For a long time, island building in the SCS on reclaimed land was being carried out by Vietnam and the Philippines, albeit on a small scale. However, after Xi Jinping became the Paramount Leader of China in March 2013, China entered the island-building game and during the period 2014–2016, it created more artificially island surface using reclaimed land, than all other nations had done so combined earlier.

China's actions in the SCS have been largely described as *Salami Slicing Strategy* or *Cabbage Wrapping Strategy*. The former strategy pertains to a series of small steps taken which overall add to a larger gain that would have either been difficult or unlawful to perform all at once. And the latter strategy involves surrounding and wrapping the islands in successive layers of Chinese naval ships and fishing boats, and cut off the targeted island from outside support.

China's Interest in Spratly Islands

Spratly Islands, named after Captain Richard Spratly, a British Sea Captain, who sighted the archipelago in the South China Sea in 1843, consists of 14 islands, six banks, 113 submerged reefs, 35 underwater banks and 21 underwater shoals. Just 45 of these geographical features are inhabited but only with military personnel from China, Taiwan, Malaysia, Vietnam and the Philippines as only these few geographical features have permanent drinking water sources in the entire archipelago. Brunei and Indonesia are the only two nations amongst the seven nations involved in disputes over the Spratly Islands that do not have any physical presence in the archipelago.

The Spratly Islands have a naturally occurring area of less than 2 square kilometres and are spread over an area of more than 425,000 square kilometre. Since they are located in strategic shipping lanes, and hence have many claimants which has often raised tempers in this picturesque region of the South China Sea.

The Spratly Islands have a unique distinction of being known by six names. Apart from its internationally known name in English, it has different names in China, Taiwan, the Philippines, Malaysia and Taiwan, thus showcasing once again how these nations strongly express their claims on this archipelago.

The seven nations involved in the dispute over the Spratly Islands have based their claims on historical rights, discovery rights, islands lying within its EEZ or being part of a nation's continental shelf.

China, being the most economically strong and militarily capable nation amongst these seven disputing nations, has been the most vocal and vociferous for the control of the Spratly Islands, which has a much deeper significance than mere physical possession of this archipelago.

There is an ambiguity in Part III, Section 2, Articles 38-39 of UNCLOS, which is being exploited by the seven disputing nations for control of the Spratly Islands. According to this particular portion of UNCLOS, the laws regarding the passage through straits require the determination of whether the straits form an island are connected to a nation's mainland. If they are not connected, ships have a right of transit passage. However, if the straits are connected to a nation, then other transit passages will be recommended, keeping in view the security of the nation in question.

In other words, UNCLOS grants the nations owning the islands or territorial sea beds a great amount of control, than the nations who depend on these sea lanes for shipping have limited influence.

Hence, China's claim over the Spratly Islands not only would result in the control of this archipelago, but also extend their sea territory all the way up to Malaysia, Indonesia, Vietnam, the Philippines and Brunei.

If China is able to get the physical possession of this archipelago, it would control almost the entire South China Sea and no other country will be able to either protest the Chinese naval activities in these waters in future or limit the economic activities in the SCS, which would include commercial shipping, fishing, oil, gas exploration, and production.

In clear and crisp words, China would become the undisputed owner of the South China Sea and later would try to extend its dominance over the Indo-Pacific region, comprising the Indian Ocean and the Pacific Ocean.

Apart from the USA, the only other four nations capable of checking and containing China's dream and desire of controlling the South China Sea are India, Taiwan, the Philippines and Vietnam.

The Spratly Islands War of 2029

After China annexes Taiwan in 2027, it is then greater alarm bells will start ringing in the White House, the office-residence of the US President, that the American folly of cosying up to China, including the blunders of the US President Richard Nixon's visit to China and diplomatically recognising China and derecognising Taiwan in 1979, were the pivotal reasons that made China annex Taiwan, and now China emboldened with the success on Taiwan, will expand its hegemonic reach over the Indo-Pacific region.

It is but obvious that the control of the South China Sea will make China control the activities of the Indo-Pacific region because of its geostrategic and geoeconomic location, like a conductor controls the symphony or an orchestra. Control of the SCS will give China unlimited powers to orchestrate the activities in the entire Indo-Pacific region from western USA to the Horn of Africa and the Cape of Good Hope.

So, after the loss of Taiwan to China in 2027, the USA will increase its presence in the South China Sea and will carry out repeated and regular military manoeuvres in this region as a show of strength, apart from levying a plethora of economic sanctions on China. These naval manoeuvres will many a time result in close contact between the PLAN and the US Navy, and close proximity flying between the United States Air Force (USAF) and PLAAF.

China on its part, will not get provoked easily after winning its war for Taiwan in 2027, as it will seek time to readjust and realign with the economic sanctions unleashed by the USA and consolidate its control over Taiwan. But, having learnt the lessons of how Russia and Iran outmanoeuvred the sanctions levied on them by the USA and the West, China will not be affected much as it would have taken many pre-emptive economic prudent measures to mitigate the effects of these economic sanctions.

Moreover, with China being a trading partner with almost all the 195 countries that exist globally, and being the largest trading partner with 120 countries, it is highly unlikely that, barring a handful of a maximum of ten countries, no country will snap its economic and diplomatic relations with China after it annexes Taiwan in 2027.

As of 2023, China exported US$ 3.38 trillion worth of goods to the international markets, while it imported US$ 2.16 trillion worth of goods. Now, with a trade figure of US$ 5.54 trillion in 2023, which will rise further by 2029, even if ten countries snap their economic and diplomatic relations with China post its Taiwan's annexation in 2027, will be nothing less than a miracle for the wishful thinking of the USA.

Despite all the hype in the international media, which is essentially controlled by the West about China's economy slumping, the latest figures speak otherwise. In February 2024, China exported US$ 220 billion worth of goods and imported US$ 181 billion, resulting in a positive trade balance of US$ 39 billion.

Between February 2023 and February 2024, the exports of China have increased by US$ 6 billion from US$ 214 billion to US$ 220 billion, making it an increase of 2.92% in percentage terms. In the same period, China's imports decreased by US$ 16 billion from US$ 197 billion to US$ 181 billion, a decrease of 8.43% in percentage terms, thus showing the increase in domestic production for domestic use.

China has officially declared reserves of US$ 3.1 trillion, though some economists have stated that China has reserves of US$ 6 trillion in foreign assets.

To further add salt to those media outlets who berate loudly about China's economic collapse, reports suggest that China has not declared US$ 3 trillion in the official banking books of the People's Bank of China. This hidden trove of money called as *Shadow Reserves*, are held by state commercial lenders and policy banks, and are said to be increasing year-on-year.

China's central role in the global economy gives it an undisputed edge that any actions it takes, visible or invisible, it will impact the rest of the world. In such a financial scenario, how many countries will dare boycott China, economically or diplomatically, is anybody's guess.

The USA itself hasn't been able to decouple from China, let alone other nations in the world. In 2023, the USA imported US$ 427.2 billion worth of goods from China. Though it is roughly 20% less than what it imported from China in 2022, but it imported US$ 475.6 billion worth of goods from Mexico, making Mexico surpass China as the biggest exporter of goods to the USA in 2023. Interestingly, most of the Mexican firms exporting to the USA are either owned by the Chinese or have huge Chinese investments in them.

Thus, directly or indirectly China will always remain the biggest exporter to the USA, as it is impractical to negate either China being the world's manufacturing hub or the immense financial clout it enjoys given its deep pockets.

With this brief financial background that China is firmly entrenched in, let us fast forward once again to 2027 after China annexes Taiwan. As the USA will increase its military manoeuvres in the South China Sea and levy a plethora of economic sanctions which will have little/no impact on China, the two-year period from 2027 to 2029 will see a large number of incidents wherein the US Navy & PLAN, and the USAF & PLAAF, will operate in close vicinity of each other's warships and fighter aircrafts.

Then in 2029, Xi Jinping will decide that enough is enough. Since the next big war that he has to fight with India is in 2035 which would also be the last war under him in his lifetime, it is imperative that the issue of Spratly Islands is put to rest once and for all. Hence, in 2029, China will physically occupy the Spratly Islands.

None of the other four countries mentioned earlier in this chapter, apart from the USA, can pose a formidable challenge to China's annexation of the Spratly Islands. Taiwan, India, Vietnam and the Philippines will not cause any worthwhile dent to the Chinese occupation of the Spratly Islands.

For, Taiwan would have ceased to exist as an independent nation in 2027, and would have physically been incorporated as the 23rd Province of China.

Vietnam and the Philippines would try naval operations to wrest back the Spratly Islands from China, but the overwhelmingly large PLA, with 1,000 nuclear weapons in its arsenal by then, would easily supress any military manoeuvres by the small militaries of Vietnam and the Philippines.

India will not be in any position to stop the annexation of the Spratly Islands by China in 2029, as it would be busy preparing itself for the two-front war that China and Pakistan will jointly wage on India in 2035.

7

Two-Front War on India

General Manoj Pande, the recently-retired 29th Chief of Army Staff (COAS) of the Indian Army, brought to the fore new domains of war, when he addressed the faculty and student officers of the Indian Armed Forces and 36 officers from foreign nations, in an address to the 79th Staff Course on April 08, 2024, in the Defence Services Staff College, India. In his address, the Indian Army Chief spoke of new domains of war including space, cyber, electromagnetic spectrum and information technology.

The General Officer further called upon the Indian Armed Forces to be always prepared for *Black Swan* events and to expect the unexpected, even as he identified technology as the new era for strategic competition among nations.

This address of the recently-retired COAS assumes immense significance in the backdrop of PLA's military doctrine a decade back of 2014, which stated that the PLA is prepared to fight any country of the world in all the six domains of war consisting of land, sea, air, cyber, electromagnetic spectrum and space, coupled with the fact that India is staring at a two-front war to be waged jointly by China and Pakistan on India in 2035.

India which is the seventh-largest country by area and the most populous nation in the world, is located in an important geostrategic location, being bounded by the Indian Ocean in the south, the Bay of Bengal in the southeast and the Arabian Sea in the southwest. Administratively, India comprises 28 states and eight union territories.

India has a 3,488 kilometres long land border with China which is called as the Line of Actual Control (LAC). With Pakistan, the land border that India has is 3,323 kilometres long called as the International Border (IB), which includes 740 kilometres called as the Line of Control (LoC). India has a total of 15,106.7 kilometres of land border and a coastline of 7,516.6 kilometres.

The Andaman and Nicobar Islands, a union territory of India, which is a group of 573 islands located in the Bay of Bengal and the headquarters of India's only Tri-Services command known as the Andaman and Nicobar Command, is located 274 kilometres from Myanmar, 193 kilometres from Indonesia and 1,078 kilometres from the Malacca Strait.

Lakshadweep Islands, another union territory of India located in the Arabian Sea is a tropical archipelago of 36 atolls and coral reefs, houses the newly inaugurated Indian Navy base INS Jatayu which was commissioned on March 06, 2024, is located 100 kilometres from Maldives and 3,212 kilometres from the Bab al-Mandab Strait.

The two operational commands of the Indian Navy are the Western Command and Eastern Command which are located at Mumbai and Vishakhapatnam respectively. The distance between Mumbai to the Gwadar port in Pakistan is 878 nautical miles and the distance between Kyaukpyu port in Myanmar to Vishakhapatnam is 793 nautical miles.

India has eight neighbours and shares a land border with six of them, while having a maritime border with two nations. India shares a land border with China in the north and northeast, Pakistan in the west, Nepal and Bhutan in the north and Bangladesh and Myanmar in the east. India has in its close vicinity Sri Lanka and Maldives, and shares a maritime border with these two closely located neighbours across the Palk Strait and the Eight Degree Channel respectively.

India's Independence and Creation of Pakistan in 1947

Before August 14, 1947, there was no nation known as Pakistan. India, then ruled by the Britishers for over 89 years directly from

1858 to 1947, and indirectly through the East India Company from 1757 to 1857, included the modern-day Pakistan and Bangladesh.

As the freedom movement in India began to gain momentum and with independence in sight, there was another movement gaining traction in the undivided India spearheaded by Muhammad Ali Jinnah, to create a separate nation named Pakistan on religious grounds.

Ironically, it was the same Muhammad Ali Jinnah who assisted Dadabhai Naoroji in nationalist politics upon his return from London after studying law, became a famous and wealthy Mumbai-based (then known as Bombay) lawyer and joined both the Indian National Congress and Muslim League, urging cooperation between the two organisations for achieving India's independence. Muhammad Ali Jinnah dismissed the potential threat of Hindu religion in India and in 1916 was instrumental in making both the Indian National Congress and the Muslim League present to the British a common set of demands known as the Lucknow Pact.

The return of Mohandas Karamchand Gandhi, an Indian lawyer who had studied law in London before moving on to South Africa for practising law for 21 years, to India in 1915 at the age of 45, changed the complexion of the freedom struggle in India much to the chagrin of Muhammad Ali Jinnah. Mohandas Karamchand Gandhi came to be known as Mahatma Gandhi since 1914, for using non-violent means to campaign for civil rights in South Africa, upon his return to India emerged as the key political figure for India's freedom movement, resulting in the marginalisation of Muhammad Ali Jinnah from the freedom struggle.

In 1920, Muhammad Ali Jinnah resigned from the Indian National Congress. In 1921, Mahatma Gandhi assumed the leadership of the Indian National Congress, and Muhammad Ali Jinnah's resentment and animosity towards Mahatma Gandhi kept on increasing so much so that at times Muhammad Ali Jinnah could barely be persuaded to be in the same room as Mahatma Gandhi was in, for various independence-related discussions.

As Mahatma Gandhi was becoming popular in India for his freedom struggle against the British, the stature of Muhammad Ali Jinnah within the Muslim League had started increasing and in the annual three day session of the Muslim League held in 1940 in Lahore, for the first time Muhammad Ali Jinnah put forward the two-nation theory based on the premise that the two religions, Hinduism and Islam could not coexist together in one nation after independence and announced his demand for creation of a separate Muslim nation, Pakistan. A resolution was passed to this effect on the last day of session which is known as the *Lahore Session*, also sometimes called as the *Pakistan Session*.

Mahatma Gandhi opposed the partition of India seeing it as contradicting his vision of unity among Indians of all religions. Several prominent Muslim leaders like Malik Khizar Hayat Tiwana, the Premier of Punjab, Maulana Hifzur Rahman, a nationalist Muslim and Maulana Syed Ata Ullah Shah Bukhari, the creator of the *Majlis-e-Ahrar-ul-Islam*, amongst many Muslims opposed the division of India to create a separate Muslim nation, Pakistan.

Despite the best efforts of Mahatma Gandhi and several prominent Hindu and Muslim leaders to ensure that an undivided India gained independence from the Britishers, Muhammad Ali Jinnah would have none of it and announced August 16, 1946, as the *Direct Action Day* which would entail the Muslim League taking direct action for a separate Muslim homeland after the British exit from India. Muhammad Ali Jinnah even warned the Indian National Congress "We do not want war. If you want war we accept your offer unhesitatingly. We will either have a divided India or a destroyed India".

On the day of August 16, 1946, and the days and weeks that followed, saw massacre and mayhem between Muslims and Hindus in Calcutta (now known as Kolkata), leaving over 4,000 persons dead. This incident is also infamously known as the *1946 Calcutta Killings*.

As communal tension continued in India, the British Prime Minister Clement Atlee appointed Lord Louis Mountbatten as India's last Viceroy, giving him the task of overseeing India's independence by June 30, 1948, with specific instructions to avoid partition and preserve a united India.

Despite his best efforts to follow the directives of Prime Minister Clement Atlee to ensure that India wasn't divided, the turbulent communal tensions in India made Lord Louis Mountbatten conclude that partition of India would have to be done.

Lord Louis Mountbatten formally proposed the partition plan of India on June 03, 1947, as violence continued unabated in India.

On July 18 1947, the British Parliament passed the *Indian Independence Act 1947*, entailing the end of the British rule in India a month later on August 15, 1947 with stipulations of creation of a new nation, Pakistan.

Cyril John Radcliffe, a British lawyer, was given the chairmanship of the two boundary committees set up after the enacting of the *Indian Independence Act 1947*, with a clear task of drawing the borders and boundaries for independent India and the newly-created nation of Pakistan that was to happen the next month in August 1947.

With only five weeks given to Cyril John Radcliffe for such an onerous task to be performed without an inkling of the far-reaching consequences that this work would have in the coming years and decades, the partition plan was submitted on August 09, 1947.

Pakistan was created as a new nation on August 14, 1947, and the next day India became independent on August 15, 1947.

Pakistan then consisted of West Pakistan on the western border of India and East Pakistan on the eastern border of India. Between West Pakistan and East Pakistan lay India.

Radcliffe's partition plan was formally announced on August 17, 1947, which saw over 14 million people displaced, when to their horror they suddenly found that they had been left in a country not of their choice. In this process, over two million people died.

The scars of the partition would continue to haunt India and Pakistan forever in the times ahead with no friendship between the two neighbouring nations, which would result not only in four conventional wars between the two hostile neighbours but over five decades of terrorism too in India and over two decades of terrorism in Pakistan.

The peace that Muhammad Ali Jinnah wanted for Pakistan as a new nation would remain elusive and would keep Pakistan on a boil, as the turn of events would reveal in the coming times.

Conflict-ridden Path of India-Pakistan Relations

As the winter chill was just setting in Jammu and Kashmir, then an independent nation, in the month of October 1947, it was just over two months that India had got independent and Pakistan created, this picturesque land would soon become one of the most hotly contested regions in the world.

Such is the beauty of the Kashmir Valley, part of Jammu and Kashmir, that Emperor Jahangir, a Mughal King in the 17th Century, part of the Mughal Empire ruling India, remarked in awe and admiration on seeing Kashmir "If there is a heaven on earth, it's here, it's here, it's here".

Prior to 1815, the area now known as Jammu and Kashmir comprised 22 small independent states of which 16 were Hindu majority and 6 were Muslim majority states. These 22 states were collectively referred to as the *Punjab Hill States*. These states were essentially vassals of the Mughal Empire. However, as the Mughal Empire declined, these hill states came under the control of the Sikh Empire led by Maharaja Ranjit Singh.

The *First Anglo-Sikh War*, fought between the East India Company and the Sikh Empire in 1845–46, resulted in the defeat of the Sikh Empire. This resulted in the East India Company asserting sovereignty over Kashmir after the *Treaty of Lahore*, which was signed on March 09, 1946, between the two warring adversaries.

Under the provisions of the *Treaty of Lahore*, the Sikhs had to surrender the Jullundur Doab area, a highly fertile region between the Beas River and the Sutlej River and also had to pay an indemnity of Rs 1.2 million.

The Sikhs were unable to raise this princely sum of money at a short notice and hence the East India Company allowed the Dogra ruler, Maharaja Gulab Singh Jamwal to purchase Kashmir by making a payment of Rs 750,000 to the East India Company.

Thus, Maharaja Gulab Singh Jamwal became the first Maharaja of Jammu and Kashmir and founded the Dogra Dynasty that would rule Jammu and Kashmir till 1947.

In 1947, as the independence of India and the creation of Pakistan was imminent, there existed 565 princely states also called as native states that were given the option of joining either India or Pakistan.

Sardar Vallabbhai Patel, who would go on to become India's first Home Minister, by his efforts persuaded 562 princely states to join India. Jammu and Kashmir under Maharaja Hari Singh, was amongst those three princely states that refused to either join India or Pakistan, the other two being Mysore and Hyderabad.

On August 20, 1947, just six days after Pakistan became a new nation, the Pakistan Army prepared a plan code-named *Operation Gulmarg* to wrest Jammu and Kashmir. According to this plan, 20 *Lashkars* (tribal militias), each consisting of 1,000 Pashtun tribesmen, were to be recruited, armed and trained for seizing Jammu and Kashmir. *Operation Gulmarg* was to be launched on October 22, 1947, with 10 *Lashkars* detailed to capture Srinagar, the winter capital of Jammu and Kashmir, and 10 *Lashkars* detailed to capture Jammu, the summer capital of Jammu and Kashmir.

As per the original planning, 10 *Lashkars* headed to seize Srinagar. They moved with ease and encountered little to no resistance as the Jammu and Kashmir State Forces were small in number, and the *Lashkars* reached Baramulla, a small town just 53.8 kilometres from Srinagar. Over confident and over joyed that now Srinagar was not too far away, the *Lashkars* started plundering the residents of Baramulla and raping the women too. Their move thus got stalled as they took to these macabre activities.

Aware of the gravity of the situation, Maharaja Hari Singh asked for assistance from India. Help was agreed to be given by India on the condition of the Maharaja signing the *Instrument of Accession* to India.

On October 26, 1947, Maharaja Hari Singh signed the *Instrument of Accession* with India and the very next day on October 27, 1947, the Indian Army landed in Srinagar and moved immediately to Baramulla where the *Lashkars* were busy plundering the town and raping the women.

The Indian Army fought hard to the last man, last round, and the *Lashkars* started retreating. A clear and total military victory for the Indian Army was on the horizon. And then India did the unexpected, by approaching the United Nations on January 01, 1948, calling upon the international body to call out Pakistan to end the aggression.

The move backfired and the United Nations, on January 20, 1948, adopted a resolution to set up the United Nations Commission for India and Pakistan (UNCIP) to establish peace in the region.

While the United Nations started working on ways and means to end the war, the war raged with greater fury between the Indian Army and the *Lashkars*, as the Pakistan Army regulars had entered the war openly in mid-1948 and the fighting intensified between the two armies.

This war lasted until January 01, 1949, when a United Nations mandated ceasefire came into effect, and resulted in 1104 fatal casualties on the Indian side and 6000 lay dead on the Pakistani side.

The UNCIP ceasefire resolution called upon Pakistan to withdraw its forces from Jammu and Kashmir and India to withdraw the bulk of its forces after the Pakistanis had withdrawn, except a bare minimum force to maintain law and order. The resolution further went on to state that the future of Jammu and Kashmir shall be determined in accordance with the will of the people.

Though the war stopped between India and Pakistan, the UNCIP ceasefire resolution was neither acceptable to India nor to Pakistan. India felt cheated by the UNCIP resolution as it had approached the United Nations with the only aim of the international body telling Pakistan to withdraw from Jammu and Kashmir. And Pakistan would have nothing less than the whole Jammu and Kashmir.

Meanwhile, as the ceasefire came into effect, India got the control of two-thirds of Jammu and Kashmir and Pakistan got the control of the remaining one-third. Clearly, by approaching the United Nations as a military victory seemed pretty much in sight, was a grave blunder that resulted in India losing one-third of Jammu and Kashmir to Pakistan.

Pakistan calls its one-third occupied portion of Jammu and Kashmir as Azad Kashmir while India terms the one-third portion illegally occupied by Pakistan, as Pakistan Occupied Jammu and Kashmir (POJK).

Also, Cease Fire Line (CFL) was created post the Karachi Agreement which was signed on July 27, 1949, between India and Pakistan in Jammu and Kashmir, which till date is monitored by United Nations observers.

After the termination of UNCIP, the Security Council of the United Nations passed Resolution 91 in 1951 and established a United Nations Military Observer Group in India and Pakistan (UNMOGIP) to monitor and report ceasefire violations.

Peace would not reign long in the Indian sub-continent after the United Nations mandated ceasefire resolution that ended the war between India and Pakistan over Jammu and Kashmir.

Pakistan clearly emboldened by capturing one-third of Jammu and Kashmir, which comprises an area of 72,935 square kilometres less 5,180 square kilometres of Shaksgam Valley, which Pakistan leased to China in 1963, was planning all the while since 1949 its next military operation to capture the balance two-third of Jammu and Kashmir comprising 1,06,566 square kilometres in India.

The opportune moment for Pakistan to launch its next military operation came when India got defeated in the 1962 India-China War also known as the Sino-Indian War or the Indo-China War, which will be discussed later in this chapter.

In 1954, Pakistan signed a defence agreement with the USA and subsequently it started receiving economic and military assistance from America from 1955. In the next one decade till 1965, Pakistan received more aid from the USA than Israel, with the aid peaking in 1962.

Economic and military assistance from the USA coupled with India's loss to China in the 1962 War, provided Pakistan the perfect cocktail to launch its next military operation against India to annex the two-third portion of Jammu and Kashmir, an integral part of India since October 26, 1947.

The planning for *Operation Gibraltar*, the codename of Pakistan's next covert overture in Jammu and Kashmir started in the mid-1950s, as an aftermath to *Operation Nusrat*, launched in 1950 for groundwork and intelligence gathering for *Operation Gibraltar*.

On August 05, 1965, about 40,000 Pakistani troops of the Azad Kashmir Regular Force commenced their crossing over to Jammu and Kashmir in India across the CFL. These troops were known as the Gibraltar Force and were commanded by Major General Akhtar Hussain Malik, General Officer Commanding (GOC) 12 Division of the Pakistan Army.

The Gibraltar Force was subdivided into 10 forces with five companies in each force. Only one out of the 10 forces, codenamed Ghaznavi Force was an auxiliary special operations unit of 200 personnel under the command of Major Malik Munawar Khan Awan.

The plan of *Operation Gibraltar* was two-pronged. Nine forces would mingle with the local populace in Jammu and Kashmir and incite them to rebel against India, while Ghaznavi Force would indulge in guerilla warfare by destroying critical infrastructure in Jammu and Kashmir. It was believed by Pakistan that the uprising in Jammu and Kashmir coupled with guerilla warfare would result in Jammu and Kashmir ceding to Pakistan, as India just from a fresh defeat from China in 1962, would neither involve itself in a full-fledged war nor would be successful in quelling the rebellion.

The Gibraltar Force after crossing the CFL, started mingling with the local populace of Jammu and Kashmir. However, none of the nine forces tasked to incite the local populace to rebel against India, achieved any success. The Ghaznavi Force too could not inflict any great damage.

The local populace of Jammu and Kashmir tipped off the Indian Army about the attempts of the Gibraltar Force and *Operation Gibraltar* ended in a whimper, as a total failure. However, Pakistan made progress in certain areas of Tithwal, Uri and Poonch while India captured the crucial Haji Pir Pass, eight kilometres inside POJK on August 28, 1965.

The failure of Operation Gibraltar was a huge setback for Pakistan and a big loss of face for the Pakistan Army, which had not even informed the Pakistan Air Force of this covert overture inside India, as it was certain of achieving success.

Desperate for success, Pakistan launched a counter-attack called *Operation Grand Slam* on September 01, 1965, with the aim of capturing the town of Akhnoor located in the strategic Chicken's Neck area which connects Jammu and Kashmir with the balance India. The Chicken's Neck area is 170 square kilometres, which is also known as the Akhnoor Dagger, whose control can give Pakistan immense strategic advantages and thus has been a focal point of all conventional wars between India and Pakistan.

Pakistan attacked Akhnoor with an overwhelming higher ratio of troops and tanks than India had anticipated. The next day, both the Indian Air Force (IAF) and the Pakistan Air Force (PAF) entered the war. Pakistan started making tactical gains in the Chicken's Neck area.

To put pressure on Pakistan, India crossed the International Border further down south on September 06, 1965. Caught unaware and completely surprised, Pakistan had no option but to pull out troops from the Chicken's Neck area to stop India's advance inside its territory across the International Border. This war witnessed some of the fiercest land and aerial battles.

On September 20, 1965, the United Nations passed a resolution demanding unconditional ceasefire from both the warring nations within 48 hours. India immediately accepted the ceasefire resolution and Pakistan accepted it on September 23, 1965.

The 1965 India-Pakistan War ended in a stalemate with no significant gains for either side that went to war. Rather the returning of the Haji Pir Pass as a consequence of the Tashkent Agreement, was a strategic blunder of India, as this geographical feature would have reduced the distance between Poonch and Uri, two important border towns of Jammu and Kashmir from 282 kilometres to just 56 kilometres. This war saw 2,862 Indian soldiers and 5,800 Pakistani soldiers dead.

An uncomfortable peace would reign in the Indian subcontinent for just six more years, before the next war between the two nations would commence once again.

West Pakistan and East Pakistan (known as East Bengal till 1955), the two portions comprising Pakistan that was created as a new nation on August 14, 1947, were separated from each other by a distance of 1600 kilometres, with India located between these two parts of Pakistan.

Bengal a province of undivided India prior to 1947, was divided into Hindu-majority West Bengal and the Muslim-majority East Bengal by the British in 1947. West Bengal remained a state in India and East Bengal became a part of Pakistan in 1947.

East Bengal was the more populous and cosmopolitan part of Pakistan, as compared to West Pakistan. East Pakistan had an area of 148,460 square kilometres while West Pakistan had an area of 881,640 square kilometres. As per the 1951 Census, East Pakistan had a population of 44.25 million while West Pakistan had a population of 33.7 million.

The clash between East and West Pakistan was evident right from start for three reasons. One, the inherent cultural distinctiveness in terms of language and culture, as East Pakistan spoke Bengali language and had a totally different culture from West Pakistan where Urdu language was spoken. Two, the West Pakistanis are traditionally dominant people, whereas East Pakistanis were soft-spoken and not aggressive in nature. And three, the huge distance of 1600 kilometres that separated the two exclaves that constituted Pakistan.

An exclave is a portion of a state geographically separated from the main part by some surrounding foreign entity. West Pakistan always considered itself as the main part of Pakistan and East Pakistan was regarded as a subordinate entity despite East Pakistan having a much larger population. This superiority attitude of West Pakistan disregarding the aspirations of East Pakistan sowed the seeds of discontentment in East Pakistan.

Soon after the creation of Pakistan, the Government of Pakistan decided in 1948 that the Urdu language will be the sole federal language of Pakistan of both West Pakistan and East Bengal. Also alternately, writing in Bengali language in the Perso-Arabic script was also introduced. This law ignited huge protests in East Bengal and the movement came to be known as the *Bengali Language Movement* also known as *Bangla Basha Andolon.*

The Government of Pakistan clamped a ban on public meetings and rallies. The tensions simmered in East Bengal and finally on February 21, 1952, the students of University of Dhaka, located in Dhaka, the capital of East Bengal, organised a public protest. The police killed student demonstrators, provoking widespread civil unrest. Finally, the Government of Pakistan unable to quell the civil unrest in East Bengal, granted official status to Bengali language in 1956.

In 1954, the Prime Minister of Pakistan, Muhammad Ali Bogra implemented the *One Unit Scheme* under which two wings of Pakistan were established, called as East Pakistan and West Pakistan. East Bengal was renamed as East Pakistan and West Pakistan was made as one political entity, which earlier was four different political identities—Punjab, Sindh, Baluchistan and North-West Frontier Province.

The *Bengali Language Movement* achieved much more than only getting official status to the Bengali language in Pakistan. It catalysed the assertion of Bengali national identity, which would become a precursor to the liberation of East Pakistan from Pakistan.

1964 saw mass riots in East Pakistan, which are also called as the *1964 East Pakistan Riots,* which saw Hindus being massacred and ethnic cleansed in the aftermath of an alleged theft of the Prophet's hair from the Hazratbal shrine in Jammu and Kashmir.

Five years later in 1969, there was a mass uprising against President Ayub Khan, a former Commander-in-Chief of the Pakistan Army who had usurped power in a coup in 1958, for his dictatorial way of functioning, in both the geographical wings of Pakistan.

Finally, as the protests against President Ayub Khan swelled with each passing day, the Pakistan President resigned on March 25,

1969 and the same day General Yahya Khan the Commander-in-Chief of the Pakistan Army, was sworn in as the next President of Pakistan.

Soon after becoming the President of Pakistan, Yahya Khan announced general elections in Pakistan. Next year in 1970, he disestablished the status of West Pakistan as a single province and restored it to four provinces that existed in the western portion of Pakistan in 1947, when Pakistan was created as a new nation.

Meanwhile, Sheikh Mujibur Rehman a prominent politician of East Pakistan spearheaded the *Six Point Movement* which comprised political, economic and military issues. However, this was unacceptable to those in Islamabad, the capital of Pakistan located in West Pakistan, as it felt that if the six points were implemented, the balance of power would shift from West Pakistan to East Pakistan.

On December 07, 1970, general elections were held in Pakistan for the first time since creation of Pakistan in 1947. Ironically, this was also the last general elections that an undivided Pakistan saw, as next year in 1971, Pakistan was dismembered into two nations.

Voting took place for 300 seats of the National Assembly, of which 162 were in East Pakistan and 138 in West Pakistan. The two main political opponents for the general elections were the west-based Pakistan People's Party (PPP) and the east-based Awami League.

In East Pakistan, the Awami League was the only reckonable political force, and in West Pakistan the PPP had severe competition from political parties like the Muslim League (Qayyum), the Jamiat Ulema-e- Islam and Jammat-e-Islami.

The results of these elections saw the Awami League getting 160 seats and the PPP getting 86 seats. These results were not acceptable to either President Yahya Khan or the PPP Chairman, Zulfikar Ali Bhutto, who did not want Pakistan being governed by a political party belonging to East Pakistan.

The inauguration of the National Assembly was delayed by the President and he tasked Nurul Amin, a Bengali Pakistani politician and jurist, to work out a compromise between PPP and the Awami League.

But the Awami League was in no mood to compromise and unrest started in East Pakistan. As the unrest grew in East Pakistan, President Yahya Khan ordered *Operation Searchlight* to quell the unrest.

The Pakistan Army formations located in East Pakistan under the command of Lieutenant General (Lt Gen) Tikka Khan, under *Operation Searchlight*, started a crackdown on the dissents on March 26, 1971, with the aim of taking control of all the cities of East Pakistan within a month and then eliminating all Bengali opposition, be it political or military.

Operation Searchlight resulted in over 3 million killed and over 10 million fled to India. Meanwhile, Mukti Bahini the guerilla resistance movement, started in East Pakistan soon after *Operation Searchlight* commenced. A civil war broke out in East Pakistan between the Pakistan Army and the Mukti Bahini.

As the genocide continued unabated by the Pakistan Army in East Pakistan and the influx of the refugees continued to India, there was no option for India but to prepare for war as all efforts of India requesting the international community to stop the genocide and influx of refugees failed.

Aleksei Alekseyevich Rodionov, the ambassador of the USSR to Pakistan, in August 1971 conveyed a secret message from the Soviet President to President Yahya Khan warning of a suicidal course for Pakistan, if it did not find a political solution to the imbroglio in East Pakistan.

But Pakistan would listen none of the advice being given and continued its genocide in East Pakistan and started preparing for a war with India.

On December 03, 1971, at about 5.35 p.m., the PAF in a preemptive airstrike codenamed *Operation Chengiz Khan*, attacked eight Indian airfields. Little later the same evening, the Prime Minister of India, Indira Gandhi in a radio broadcast announced that the Pakistani airstrikes were a declaration of war on India and that India would give a befitting reply.

Soon after the radio broadcast of the Indian Prime Minister, the Indian Armed Forces launched *Operation Vijay* and a full-scale military offensive was launched both in East Pakistan and West Pakistan simultaneously.

General SHFJ Manekshaw, the Chief of Army Staff of the Indian Army, had made fool-proof war plans and the blitzkrieg ground operations of the Indian Army duly supplemented by the IAF and the Indian Navy working in tandem, took the Pakistan Army in East Pakistan by surprise and shock.

In a four-pronged offensive the Indian Army encircled Dhaka in just 13 days into the war and the Pakistan Army surrendered to the Indian Army. In this war between the two neighbours, 3843 Indian soldiers died while 9000 Pakistani soldiers were killed. 93,000 Pakistani soldiers were captured as Prisoners of War (POW) by India. On December 16, 1971, India declared military victory over Pakistan and East Pakistan was renamed Bangladesh and a new nation emerged in the Indian subcontinent.

Pakistan was dismembered into two nations and the message of Aleksei Alekseyevich Rodionov, the ambassador of the USSR to Pakistan conveyed a few months before in August 1971, proved prophetically correct.

After Pakistan's split into two nations in late December 1971, Pakistan realised that it would be near impossible to defeat the Indian Armed Forces in a conventional war in future. As a result, two important things happened in Pakistan regarding its action against India. One, planned, and the other, unexpected.

The planned action was the formulation of the *Bleed India with a Thousand Cuts Military Doctrine* in Pakistan and the unexpected happening was China's extreme closeness to Pakistan after Xi Jinping became the Paramount Leader of China in March 2013, which has already been discussed in detail in Chapter 4 of the book.

As part of the *Bleed India with a Thousand Cuts Military Doctrine*, the Chief of Army Staff of the Pakistan Army, General Zia-ul-Haq in 1976 propounded that since it was not possible for Pakistan to defeat India in any conventional war, Pakistan should aid and abet terrorism and covert operations, so that India starts getting unstable internally, and when the time is ripe, then Pakistan should attack India to seize Jammu and Kashmir. This military doctrine is till date taught to the officers of the Pakistan Armed Forces undergoing the staff course, which is an important mid-career course for the officers of Pakistan Army, Navy and the Air Force, in Staff College, Quetta.

The next year, in 1977, General Zia-ul-Haq in a coup de état overthrew Zulfikar Ali Bhutto, the Pakistani Prime Minister and seized power. This military doctrine got a fillip with General Zia-ul-Haq's presidency and for its implementation efforts got underway.

Pakistan did not have to wait for long to put this military doctrine to use, and the emergence of the Khalistan movement in the Indian state of Punjab, gave Pakistan the perfect testbed for carrying out the implementation of this doctrine. The Khalistanis, with Pakistani aid, started carrying out terrorist activities in Punjab demanding for a separate nation called Khalistan. For over 15 years that terrorism lasted in Punjab from 1980 to 1995, over 15,000 Indian security personnel and citizens died and over 6000 Khalistani terrorists were killed.

As terrorism was waning in Punjab in the end-1990s, Pakistan opened a new internal terrorism front in Jammu and Kashmir. It has been over 35 years that terrorism started in Jammu and Kashmir on July 13, 1989, continues to this day. Over 7000 Indian security forces personnel and 20,000 citizens have died so far in Jammu and Kashmir due to the Pakistan sponsored terrorism, and over 26,000 terrorists have been killed till now.

Amidst the sponsoring of terrorism in Jammu and Kashmir, Pakistan launched its fourth conventional war on India, known as the Kargil War in 1999, militarily known as *Op Koh Paima* in Pakistan and *Op Vijay* in India.

Operation (Op) Koh Paima was the name given by the General Headquarters (GHQ) of the Pakistan Army to an operation planned by the Kargil Clique, comprising Gen Pervez Musharraf, the COAS, Lt Gen Aziz Khan, the Chief of General Staff, Lt General Mahmud, GOC 10 Corps and Brig Javed Hassan, Commander Force Command Northern Area, to take over certain territories in the Kargil sector of Jammu and Kashmir in India in a well-planned and secrecy-shrouded military operation. Koh Paima in Urdu means one who climbs a mountain.

Op Koh Paima was planned because of the four main reasons— to capitalise on the Pakistan's nuclear tests in 1998, the weakening of insurgency in Jammu and Kashmir, growing insecurity in the Pakistani military establishment due to the increasing closeness between the Prime Ministers of India and Pakistan—Atal Bihari Vajpayee and Nawaz Sharif—and the fear amongst Pakistan Army Generals of the weakening of the Kashmir factor and the omission of the 'Kashmir' word from the Lahore Declaration.

Op Koh Paima was approved by the Pakistani COAS on January 16, 1999, less than five weeks before the signing of the historic Lahore Declaration by the Prime Ministers of India and Pakistan on February 22, 1999. The move by the Pakistani Army to occupy the territories in the Kargil sector began soon thereafter.

It was for the first time on May 17, 1999, that the Pakistani Prime Minister, Nawaz Sharif, was briefed about Op Koh Paima by the Director General Military Operations (DGMO) of the GHQ. By then the Pakistani troops were well entrenched inside the Indian territory. In attendance were also the Pakistani Chief of Air Staff and the Chief of Naval Staff who were equally dumbfounded to hear the presentation, as they too, like the civilian leadership, were absolutely clueless of the overtures planned and executed by the Pakistani Army.

This briefing to the civilian leadership of Pakistan was necessitated because the cover of *Op Koh Paima* had been blown away, and diplomatic pressure on Pakistan was imminent. Now the Kargil Clique wanted political and diplomatic cover for *Op Koh Paima*.

The Pakistani DGMO further, in the briefing, gave four assumptions on which he guaranteed the success of *Op Koh Paima*. First was that each post occupied by the Pakistanis on the Indian soil was impregnable. Secondly, the Indians lacked the will to retaliate. Thirdly, there would be no international pressure on Pakistan to end the conflict soon. And lastly, the Pakistani Army would not ask for any additional resources form the Pakistan Government in view of the economic crunch being faced by the country.

However, that was not to be, and the entire GHQ, including their COAS and the DGMO, had grossly miscalculated the Indian response and retaliation and the international isolation that Pakistan would face because of *Op Koh Paima*.

It was in the second week of May 1999 that the Indian Army detected the presence of the Pakistanis on their soil. In the last week of May 1999, the Indian Army realised that *Op Koh Paima* was a well-orchestrated military overture. On May 26, 1999, the Indian Air Force was pressed into operations.

On May 27, 1999, 12 the Indian Armed Forces launched *Operation Vijay* to push back the Pakistani Army from its soil. Vijay in Hindi means Victory.

Thus, started the full counter-offensive by the Indian Army to thwart the designs of the Pakistani Army, which by now the whole world saw in shock as India and Pakistan, both being nuclear nations were now just a nuclear attack away. Repercussions of such a catastrophe would not only affect the Indian sub-continent but the world at large. The world watched with baited breadth as the armies of the two nuclear nations fought in the tough and the treacherous terrains of Kargil.

The Kargil War lasted from May 03 to July 26, 1999 and saw 527 Indian soldiers and 1600 Pakistani soldiers killed in action, resulting in victory for the Indian Army who vacated every inch of their land from the Pakistani Army.

As mentioned earlier, terrorism is still alive in Jammu and Kashmir though there has been a vast improvement in the security in the region after Article 370 and 35A, which gave special perks and privileges to Jammu and Kashmir, were abrogated on August 05, 2019. In 2023, there were 13 civilians killed by terrorists in Jammu and Kashmir, while 26 Indian security personnel were killed in action, and 72 terrorists were killed in the same period as compared to 86 civilians, 95 security personnel and 271 terrorists dying in 2018.

Thus, with a bloody past and ongoing terrorism in Jammu and Kashmir, one thing clearly that stands out: is Pakistan's obsession for Jammu and Kashmir. With such turbulent past, the future between India and Pakistan will not be peaceful, as the timelines would reveal, which shall be discussed later in this chapter.

Uneasy India-China relations

If the Western India bordering Pakistan has remained turbulent since India's independence in 1947, the eastern border with China too has not seen peace since the end of the Chinese Civil War in 1949.

Ironically, whereas India–Pakistan relations have remained turbulent since the creation of Pakistan and the independence of India in 1947, the relations between India and China were peaceful for thousands of years of recorded history, till 1949.

Thus, India is located in the most tough geostrategic location in the world with two hostile neighbours on its western and eastern borders.

Since ancient times India and China had sound economic and cultural relations. The *Silk Route* an ancient trade route active from the second century BCE till the mid-15th century, apart from being the major trade route was also instrumental in the spread of Buddhism from India to East Asia.

Much before India's independence in 1947, India's prominent freedom fighter who would later become India's first Prime Minister, Pandit Jawaharlal Nehru and ROC's President Chiang Kai-shek shared a long bond of friendship.

In 1939, as the Republic of China's honoured guest, Pandit Jawaharlal Nehru praised Chiang Kai-shek and his wife Song Meiling for their stellar leadership. During this visit, one night, when the Japanese bombers attacked Chongqing, Jawaharlal Nehru and Chiang Kai-shek spent the entire night in a bunker as the air raids continued in full force and fury. In return, Chiang Kai-shek visited the British-ruled India in 1942 and met the prominent Indian leaders fighting for India's independence—Mahatma Gandhi and Pandit Jawaharlal Nehru—and assured them of full support for India's independence. On the other hand, Chiang Kai-shek, a visionary leader, opposed Muhammed Ali Jinnah's call for a separate nation to be carved out of India for Muslims.

However, Pandit Jawaharlal Nehru's attitude towards Chiang Kai-shek changed drastically following India's independence in 1947, and the retreat of the Republic of China to Taiwan after the Chinese Civil War. Then, he cold-shouldered Chiang Kai-shek to move closer to communist China, for the fear that China would ferment domestic communist unrest in India.

In 1947, soon after its independence, India recognised the ROC but on April 01, 1950, it decided to switch its recognition to PRC as part of the *One China Policy* that was gaining traction globally, which India officially follows till date. India was the first non-communist/socialist nation in Asia to officially recognise the PRC.

The Indian Prime Minister Jawaharlal Nehru and the Chinese Premier Zhou Enlai shared cordial relations, and co-propounded the *Five Principles of Peaceful Coexistence* also known as *Panchsheel*.

However, the historically good relations between India and China would not last much longer and soon the two nations would become sworn enemies of each other.

After China annexed Tibet in 1950, India informed China that it did not seek any special privileges in Tibet; however, the traditional trading rights must continue. On April 29, 1954, India and China signed the *Agreement on Trade and Intercourse Between Tibet Region of China and India*, also known as the *1954 Sino-Indian Agreement* or the *Panchsheel Agreement*. This agreement, on one hand made India recognise Tibet as part of China, and on the other hand, China accepted the continuance of all previous trade agreements between India and Tibet.

Till the mid-1950s the relations between China and India were extremely cordial where the catchphrase *Hindi-Chini Bhai-Bhai* (Indians and Chinese are brothers) was often used to showcase the strong relations between the two neighbours.

However, after signing the 1954 agreement with China, India became wary of China's designs on its territories and it published maps defining its borders with China based on the McMahon Line signed in the 1914 Shimla Convention, attended by British officials ruling India, Tibetan, and Chinese officials. In January 1959, the Chinese Premier Zhou Enlai wrote a letter to the Indian Prime Minister Jawaharlal Nehru stating that the McMahon Line as a demarcation of the borders between India and China, had no legal sanctity for China. Also, he wrote that the Aksai Chin in northern India was an integral part of China. The tensions between China and India started increasing as a consequence of this letter.

From the Chinese perspective, the 3488 kilometres long LAC, the border between India and China, is divided into three sectors – Western, Middle and Eastern Sector.

- The Western Sector is the region of Ladakh on the Indian side and the Xinjiang and western Tibet regions on the Chinese side.

- The Middle Sector comprises the Indian states of Uttrakhand, Himachal Pradesh and Sikkim and the middle portion of Tibet of China.

- The Eastern Sector encompasses south Tibet of China and the Indian state of Arunachal Pradesh. This sector has the McMahon Line.

Tensions between the two neighbours further deteriorated when in March 1959, the Dalai Lama, the spiritual and temporal head of Tibet, fled to India and was accorded political asylum in India. Thereafter, started a series of violent skirmishes between the two neighbours.

The summer of 1961 saw aggressive patrolling by China across the Indian state of Arunachal Pradesh, with the Chinese patrols crossing the McMahon Line many times. To thwart these overtures, Jawaharlal Nehru formulated the *Forward Policy* under which numerous outposts were created by the Indian Army along its border with China.

On October 02, 1962, the Soviet First Secretary, Nikita Khrushchev defended Jawaharlal Nehru in a discussion he was having with Mao Zedong. This further infuriated Mao, as this was the time when the USSR–China relations were on a low. With war clouds already darkening between India and China, Mao Zedong now decided that war was the only option.

In the backdrop of the *Cuban Missile Crisis* that was underway between the USA and the USSR, China extracted a promise from the USSR that it would not intervene in case of a military confrontation between China and India, and the USSR agreed. The stage was now well-prepared by China for a war with India.

Few days later China attacked India. The *Indo-China War* also known as the *Sino-Indian War* was fought from October 20 to November 21, 1962, in the western Sector and eastern Sector of China which corresponds to the northern and eastern parts of India.

On October 20, 1962, China launched a two-pronged attack on India, inter-se separated by 1,000 kilometres in the western and eastern theatre. The western theatre saw the aggression by China in Aksai Chin and the eastern theatre saw the attack by China in Arunachal Pradesh.

By October 24, 1962, the PLA entered as much as 60 kilometres deep inside the Indian territory at some places, despite the Indian Army putting up a brave resistance despite infrastructural and logistical handicaps. Then Zhou Enlai ordered the PLA to stop its advance and then wrote a letter to Jawaharlal Nehru proposing a negotiated settlement of the borders, which included both sides withdrawing 20 kilometres from present lines of actual control, full Chinese withdrawal in Arunachal Pradesh and holding on the present lines of control in Aksai Chin.

However, Jawaharlal Nehru, in his October 27, 1962 reply to Zhou Enlai, expressed desire of restoration of peace amongst the two nations at war and suggested a pull-back to the borders that existed prior to September 08, 1962.

Zhou Enlai is his November 04, 1962, counter-reply to Jawaharlal Nehru's letter, repeated his 1959 offer of return to the McMahon Line in Arunachal Pradesh and the MacDonald Line in Aksai Chin. However, once again, Jawaharlal Nehru in his November 14, 1962, reply to Zhou Enlai latest letter, rejected the offer given by the Chinese Premier.

The same day, after receiving Jawaharlal Nehru's reply and a three-week lull in the war, Zhou Enlai ordered the PLA to resume the war. PLA reached the important Indian town of Tezpur in the eastern sector and made significant advances in the western sector and reached the line that Chinese claimed in Aksai Chin.

Elated by PLA's success, on November 19, 1962, Zhou Enlai ordered a unilateral ceasefire effective November 21, 1962, and directed the PLA in the eastern sector to withdraw 20 kilometres behind the line of control that existed between India and China on November 07, 1959.

The war between India and China that lasted from October 20 to November 21, 1962, saw 722 Chinese soldiers and 1,383 Indian soldiers being killed in action.

India lost the war with China despite the bravery shown by its officers and soldiers, due to not anticipating the Chinese intentions, lack of military preparedness and not using the Indian Air Force.

The myth *Hindi-Chini Bhai-Bhai* (Indians and Chinese are brothers) had been shattered forever and China occupied Aksai Chin in eastern Ladakh, an area of approximately 38,000 square kilometres, which is of strategic importance to China as it connects its two provinces – Xinjiang and Tibet.

The uneasy calm between India and China after the end of the 1962 war would not last long, and five years later, the *Nathu La and Cho La Clashes* also known as the *Indo-China War of 1967* occurred.

After the defeat of India in the 1962 war, seven mountain divisions were raised in the Indian Army for deployment along its border with China for times of an eventuality. Barring one mountain division deployed at Chumbi Valley on the Sikkim-Tibet border, the other six mountain divisions were located deep inside the Indian hinterland.

Sikkim at that time was an independent nation ruled by Chogyals of the Namgyal dynasty and was a Protectorate of India from 1950 to 1975. On May 16, 1975, Sikkim became a part of India after 97%

of the electorate voted for a merger with Indian in a special referendum held in Sikkim on April 14, 1975.

The Chumbi Valley, located at an altitude of 9,800 feet, is a valley in the Himalayas that projects out from the Tibetan plateau, intervening between Sikkim and Bhutan. It is coextensive with Yadong County in Tibet and is connected to Sikkim to the southwest by the mountain passes of Nathu La and Jelep La.

At Nathu La, the Indian and Chinese soldiers were located at an eyeball-to-eyeball contact, a military jargon meaning location in close proximity. The Chinese were on the northern shoulder of the Nathu La pass, and the Indians at the southern shoulder.

The tensions at Nathu La had been brewing right after the deployment of the Indian mountain division after the end of the 1962 war. On September 11, 1967, a scuffle broke out between the Indian and Chinese soldiers over laying of fencing on the Sikkim side, resulting in the Chinese opening up fire with their medium machine guns. Soon the duel increased with artillery opening up from both the sides. This clash or war lasted from September 11–14, 1967, and resulted in 65 Indian soldiers being killed, while 340 Chinese soldiers died and the Chinese had to beat a hasty retreat after a ceasefire was announced.

Barely a fortnight of uncomfortable peace had passed when on October 01, 1967, the PLA soldiers again instigated a clash with the Indian soldiers, after entering Sikkim. The Chinese were once again beaten back and 36 Indian soldiers died in this clash while the exact number of Chinese soldiers killed in this clash are unknown to date. This clash lasted for just a day.

Thus, India had avenged their 1962 war defeat from China in this both these short but high-casualty clashes/wars fought in the frosty heights of Sikkim at Nathu La and Cho La.

Peace would reign between India and China for two nearly two decades after the Cho La clash in 1967. During this period, China was itself embroiled in an internal turmoil known as *The Cultural*

Revolution which has been discussed in Chapter 2 of the book, hence its animosity with India took a backseat.

However, after *The Cultural Revolution* ended in China and its economic growth started, the tensions with India started increasing. The next location of the tensions between India and China was Arunachal Pradesh in 1986, and this clash would be known as the *Sumdorong Chu Standoff.*

In 1980, India decided that to defend the town of Arunachal Pradesh from a future Chinese aggression, the line of defence along the Hathung La Ridge would be of vital importance. As a consequence of this decision, an Intelligence Bureau team of India started going every summer to the pasturage of Sumdorong Chu, located northeast of the confluence of Namka Chu and Nyamjiang Chu, and would stay put there till the onset of winters and then return. This procedure continued till 1985.

In the summers of 1986 when the Intelligence Bureau team of India reached Sumdorong Chu, it was taken aback to see the Chinese already stationed there in semi-permanent structures.

General S. Sundarji, the COAS of the Indian Army ordered airlift of Indian Army soldiers to Zemithang on October 18, 1986, just before the onset of winters under *Operation Falcon.* The troop buildup by India took place over the next three days and was completed on October 20, 1986, and the Indian Army occupied the higher reaches overlooking Sumdorong Chu.

In response to *Operation Falcon,* China too mobilised the PLA in this area, and the standoff continued till May 1987, with tempers running high in this intervening period and the possibility of a war not being ruled out. During this period India changed the status of Arunachal Pradesh from a Union Territory to a State, which further infuriated the Chinese.

However, this time there were no casualties on either side, and the *Sumdorong Chu Standoff* ended without any bloodshed.

The major fallout of the bloodless *Sumdorong Chu Standoff* was that both India and China realised the danger of such an inadvertent conflict which had nearly resulted in a war. Hence, both the neighbours decided to have peace, amongst them, though the reasons of seeking peace by either China or India were different.

China wanted peace after the 1987 *Sumdorong Chu Standoff* was because it was on its upward trajectory of economic prosperity, and India wanted peace because of the political turmoil happening in India.

In 1988, the Indian Prime Minister Rajiv Gandhi visited China, the first Indian Prime Minister to do so after the 1962 Indo-China War, thus thawing the frosty India–China relations.

On September 07, 1993, India and China signed the *Border Peace and Tranquillity Agreement* (BPTA) during Indian Prime Minister P.V. Narasimha Rao's visit to China. Under this agreement, the border between India and China was designated as the Line of Actual Control (LAC), apart from various other provisions like reducing force levels and resolving issues related to the crisscrossing of the patrol routes.

Four more agreements for peace on the LAC were signed between India and China subsequent to BPTA in 1993. In 1996, the Agreement on Military Confidence Building Measures was signed, and in 2005, the Protocol for the Implementation of Military Confidence Measures was inked. In 2012, the Establishment of a Working Mechanism for Consultation and Coordination on India-China Border Affairs Agreement, while in 2013, the Indo-China Border Defence Cooperation Agreements were signed. However, the BPTA remained the mother of all subsequent border agreements between India and China.

But the cordial relations between India and China would not last for more than three decades, and the next major confrontation between the two neighbours would result exactly 30 years later in the form of *Doklam Standoff* in 2017, and this would happen four years after Xi Jinping would become the Paramount Leader of

China in 2013, and three years after, the *Doklam Standoff,* the *Galwan Valley Clash* in 2020 would take place.

As has been discussed earlier in Chapter 4 of the book, Xi Jinping after becoming China's Paramount Leader in 2013, realised that with the enormous economic power that China had, the time was now ripe to realise China's military ambitions.

With Aksai Chin of India already in China's control since 1962, the target now on China's radar to annex from India is Arunachal Pradesh.

Two-Front War by China and Pakistan on India

The roadmap for China's aggressive overtures towards India after three decades of peace from 1987 to 2017 was laid in 2007, when China became the world's third-biggest economy. Now it was clear to the Chinese leadership that apart from the vast economic power that China was wielding, the time was opportune to show its assertive designs too.

China has a land border of 22,117 kilometres, and until few years back, had border disputes with all the 14 nations that it shares its borders with. However, barring Bhutan and India, China has resolved the border disputes with all the other 12 countries. The China–Bhutan talks for resolving the border issues between these two countries are in an advanced stage and the settlement between China and Bhutan can be expected anytime.

It is only India with which China's border issues are not resolved and is unlikely to be resolved anytime soon, as China stakes claim over the entire Indian state of Arunachal Pradesh, which obviously is unacceptable to India. Hence for China, the only option for annexing Arunachal Pradesh from India is go to war with India and the timelines for the next war to be waged by China on India, is in 2035.

The next time that China will wage a war on India, it will not do so alone. The 2035 war will be a two-front war, waged jointly by China and Pakistan on India with Pakistan attacking India for

Jammu and Kashmir and China attacking India for annexing Arunachal Pradesh.

Before the 2035 two-front war is discussed in detail, it is important to discuss the *Doklam Standoff* in 2017 and the *Galwan Valley Clash* in 2020, both of which occurred between China and India after Xi Jinping's ascendancy to power in 2013.

Doklam is a disputed area between China and Bhutan, which is located near the tri-junction with India. China claims Doklam based on the 1890 Convention of Calcutta agreement between China and Britain. Though India doesn't have any territorial designs on Doklam, but it supports Bhutan on this issue, as India and Bhutan are signatories to the Friendship Treaty signed between the two countries in 2007.

China in the early 2000s, constructed a road up to the Sinchela Pass in the undisputed territory and then stealthily built the road over the Doklam Plateau, reaching upto 68 metres to the Indian border post in Sikkim. And in 2005, the Chinese constructed a U-turn for its vehicles to turn back.

On June 16, 2017, the PLA with construction equipment began extending the existing road southward on the Doklam Plateau. On June 29, 2017, Bhutan objected to this road-building. This area is on the Jampheri Ridge within Bhutan, and the Chinese reaching here would have given them an unhindered visibility to the strategic Siliguri Corridor, also called as the Chicken's Neck, which is 20–22 kilometres wide at the narrowest section and connects the northeast India to the balance of India.

Thus, India has two Chickens' Neck. One in the north with connects Jammu and Kashmir with the balance of India, on which Pakistan has its eyes on, which has been discussed earlier in this chapter. And the other Chicken's Neck is in eastern India, which has been described above, and on which China has its eye on.

The Indian Army on June 18, 2017, sent 270 soldiers with weapons and bulldozers to thwart the Chinese designs to construct the road. On June 29, 2017, after Bhutan objected to China building its road to the Jampheri Ridge, China the same day released a map showing Doklam as part of China.

The *Doklam Standoff* lasted for 73 days till August 28, 2017, with finally status quo prevailing and troops withdrawing to the lines of deployment that existed earlier as on June 16, 2017, when the standoff began.

Barely three years had passed since the *Doklam Standoff* ended in 2017, and at the peak of the Covid-19 pandemic that had engulfed the entire world in early 2020, started incursions into the Ladakh region of India by China in early-April 2020 who had got infuriated by India's decision to abrogate Article 370 & 35A which had given special status to the Indian state of Jammu and Kashmir. As a consequence of this legislation, Jammu and Kashmir was bifurcated into two Union Territories – Jammu and Kashmir and Ladakh. The revised maps of India showed Aksai Chin as the integral part of the newly carved union territory Ladakh.

Also, it is pertinent to mention here is that during the intervening period of Xi Jinping becoming the next Paramount Leader of China in 2013 until mid-2020, two important US-India defence deals were inked: Logistics Exchange Memorandum Agreement (LEMOA) in 2016, and the Communications Compatibility and Security Agreement (COMCASA) in 2018.

A little later, two more important defence agreements between India and USA were signed which were the Basic Exchange and Cooperation Agreement (BECA) on October 20, 2020, and the United States–India Initiative on Critical and Emerging Technology (iCET) which was signed in May 2022.

Earlier, the General Security of Military Information Agreement (GSOMIA) had been signed between USA and India in 2002.

However, the two foundational defence agreements between USA and India, namely the LEMOA in 2016 and COMCASA in 2018 coupled with India's abrogation of Article 370 and 35A in Jammu and Kashmir in 2019, set the stage for the next bloody Chinese intrusion in India after the last violent incursion in Nathu La and Cho La in 1967. This was the *Galwan Valley Clash* of 2020, and after this bloody exchange, the relations between China and India would nose dive for a long time and the tensions will eventually culminate in the two-front war in 2035.

Despite the Chinese President Xi Jinping and the Indian Prime Minister Narendra Modi meeting 18 times after the both came to power in 2013 and 2014 respectively, China decided that it was time to retaliate violently as the pressure of the two foundational defence agreements between USA and India, and the abrogation of Article 370 and 35A was surmounting on China.

In early April 2020, two divisions of the PLA under the Western Theatre Command started moving towards the LAC opposite to the eastern Ladakh region of India. On May 05, 2020, the first clash between the PLA and the Indian Army soldiers occurred at the beach of Pangong Tso, a huge lake through which the LAC passes and both the neighbours own a portion of the lake. Five days later on, May 10, 2020, another clash took place in which the soldiers of both the armies sustained injuries.

On May 21, 2020, the PLA entered the Galwan River Valley and objected to construction by India of a road in the Indian territory, and pitched 80 tents in the area, which was followed by more troop induction.

Three days later on May 24, 2020, the PLA entered India at three more places at Hot Springs, Patrol Point 14 and Patrol Point 15. India also started beefing ups their troops to block any further advance by the PLA.

On June 15, 2020, a patrol of the Indian Army in the Galwan River Valley was ambushed by the PLA. Till this time both the PLA and the Indian Army soldiers used to not carry any weapons as a result of the 1993 BPTA. In accordance with the 27-year-old adage, both the sides were carrying rods and clubs but no weapons. However, the PLA soldiers had the rods and clubs embedded in nails and barbed wire.

During the ambush of the Indian Army patrol by the PLA in the Galwan River Valley on June 15, 2020, hand-to-hand combat broke out and more troops were called in for reinforcements by both the sides.

This hand-to-hand combat which took place in the cover of darkness and lasted for six hours, resulted in 20 Indian and 40 PLA soldiers being killed in action. 10 Indian soldiers were taken captive by the PLA and were later released on June 18, 2020.

After 53 years, blood flowed on the India–China border called the LAC. Also, India lost access to 26 out of the 65 Patrolling Points in eastern Ladakh as per a news report published in *The Hindu*, a leading newspaper of India, on January 24, 2023.

Tensions and turbulence between India and China have never reduced since the *Galwan Valley Clash* of June 15, 2020, despite 21 level of Corps Commander level-talks being held between the two neighbours since the *Galwan Valley Clash*, and about 60,000 soldiers of both the armies deployed in an eyeball-to-eyeball contact in eastern Ladakh since then. The 21st Corps Commander level-meeting was held at the Chushul-Moldo border meeting point on February 19, 2024, but as always earlier these talks failed to break the impasse between the two nations.

Xi Jinping has made clear his intentions towards India by the *Galwan Valley Clash*, that neither will China vacate any inch of Aksai Chin, nor will China stop aiming for its next target on the Indian soil—Arunachal Pradesh.

Arunachal Pradesh, known earlier as the North-East Frontier Agency (NEFA), is an Indian state located in its northeast, which was a union territory after India's independence till February 20, 1987, when it became a state of India.

India has two types of administrative divisions – union territory and state. A union territory is administered directly by the Central

Government through a nominated functionary, called as the Lieutenant Governor or the Administrator. A state has an elected government and is run by a Chief Minister.

NEFA was renamed Arunachal Pradesh on January 20, 1972, and has an area of 83,743 square kilometres and a population of 1.57 million as on July 01, 2023. It has borders with China in the north, Myanmar in the east and Bhutan in the west. This largest Indian state amongst the seven northeastern states of India in terms of area, has a 1,129 kilometres long border with China which is also called as the McMahon Line.

Arunachal Pradesh means the *Land of Dawn-Lit Mountains* and has 26 major tribes and 100 sub-tribes. China claims the entire Indian state of Arunachal Pradesh as South Tibet.

China has its eyes set on Arunachal Pradesh for three important reasons –

- **Threat to East China**: As described in Chapter 1 of the book, eastern China is of immense importance to China as majority of the Chinese population and almost all-important towns and cities of China are in its eastern part. The aerial distance from Arunachal Pradesh to Beijing is 3,790 kilometres, while the distance from Leh to Beijing is 9,007 kilometres. The maximum range of the Indian missiles is 5,500 kilometres for the Agni-V (MIRV) set of missiles. Thus, if these missiles are deployed in Arunachal Pradesh, India can easily target any Chinese town or city in its eastern part. Hence, the danger to eastern China is only from Arunachal Pradesh of India and not from any other northern or eastern state of India.

- **Next Dalai Lama**: It is widely believed that the next Dalai Lama, who will succeed the incumbent 14th Dalai Lama, will be from Arunachal Pradesh. The Dalai Lama is the highest spiritual leader and head of Tibetan Buddhism. The 14th Dalai Lama is living in exile in India since 1959, when he fled to India from Tibet and currently resides in Dharamshala, in the western Indian state of Himachal Pradesh. China believes that if the 15th Dalai Lama is anointed from Arunachal Pradesh, it will likely cause an uprising amongst the Tibetans living in Tibet against China. With Arunachal Pradesh located contiguous to Tibet and the 15th Dalai Lama belonging to this area, the Tibetan uprising in the times ahead will be difficult to contain.

- **Ancestry**: China believes that the three major tribes of Arunachal Pradesh namely Tagin, Nyishi and Galo, have ancestors from Tibet and since they are now located in Arunachal Pradesh, so China exerts an historical claim over Arunachal Pradesh on this basis.

Interestingly, till 2007, China showed no great interest in Arunachal Pradesh. In fact, after China's win over India in the 1962 war, it withdrew back from NEFA, as Arunachal Pradesh was known then, despite entering as much as 60 kilometres inside India at some places in this area.

After the 1962 war, while China did not withdraw from Aksai Chin in its western sector, it did so from Arunachal Pradesh in its eastern sector, thus showing clearly that it did not accord much importance to the occupation of Arunachal Pradesh that time.

Rather, it is widely believed that until 2007, China's occasional raising of the Arunachal Pradesh was more to use it is a bargaining chip with India to gain India's recognition of Aksai China as a part of China, in turn of China's recognition of Arunachal Pradesh being part of India. This is exactly what Zhou Enlai had proposed in his November 04, 1962 letter to Jawaharlal Nehru.

However, China's attitude towards India on the Arunachal Pradesh changed drastically after it became the world's third-biggest economy in 2007. With deep pockets that China was now sitting with, it felt that it was time to make it clear to India about its reversal of intentions over Arunachal Pradesh.

From 2009 onwards, on some occasions, China started issuing stapled visas to the residents of Arunachal Pradesh desirous of visiting China for any purpose, be it tourist, business or official. This was a clear signal from China that it no longer recognises Arunachal Pradesh as an integral part of India. A stapled visa is different from a regular visa in the sense that the country issuing stapled visas does not stamp the visa on the passport of the individual, rather a paper slip visa is stapled to the passport.

In 2010 China became the world's second-biggest economy, and it was now decided by the Chinese leadership that its economic, and hence its military rise should be showcased to the world in general and the USA and India in specific, for the two main adversaries in the Chinese eyes are the USA and India.

In July 2010, China refused visa to Lt Gen BS Jaswal, GOC-in-C Northern Command of the Indian Army, who was to lead a military delegation to China, as that time the General Officer was posted in Jammu and Kashmir. China thus had conveyed to India in a subtle manner its withdrawal of recognition of the Indian state of Jammu and Kashmir too.

Later that year, in 2010, India realised that China meant business and decided to raise a Mountain Strike Corps for the Indian Army, whose role would be on the LAC against China. 17 Corps was raised on January 01, 2014 which was initially supposed to have two divisions. However, due to budgetary constraints only one division has been raised till date. Taking into consideration the heightened India–China tensions it has been widely reported in the Indian media on April 14, 2024, that the second division of 17 Corps will be raised by the end of 2024.

On October 05, 2011, General VK Singh the Indian Army Chief, stated that around 4,000 PLA soldiers were stationed in POJK. Just a year before, in 2010, the presence of over 11,000 PLA soldiers in the Gilgit-Baltistan had been sighted. Clearly, China was on an overdrive to increase its troop strength in POJK and Gilgit-Baltistan, though both these areas are under the Pakistani control.

The tensions between China with both the USA and India were now incrementally increasing after the rise of China as the world's second-largest economy in 2010.

Alongside, China's aggressiveness in the South China Sea was increasing, leading to the US Secretary of State, Hillary Clinton remarking at the ASEAN Regional Forum Meeting in Hanoi on July 23, 2010, that the importance of freedom of navigation in the SCS was a vital American national interest and the region should be open for normal commercial shipping. China, on expected lines protested and continued its activities in the SCS undeterred.

On December 21, 2011, the US President Barack Obama announced the *East Asia Strategy* also known as *Pivot to Asia*, whereby the American focus was shifted from the Middle East and Europe to the Indo-Pacific Region to counter China's rise as a rival superpower. The six stated objectives of this strategy included strengthening bilateral security alliances, deepening America's relationships with rising powers including China, engaging with regional multilateral institutions, expanding trade and investment, forging a broad-based military presence and advancing democracy and human rights. Also, under this strategy, majority of the US troops stationed in the Middle East were moved to the Indo-Pacific Region in a gradual and calibrated manner.

To checkmate the USA's *East Asia Strategy* which had the sure potential of playing a spoiler in not only China's control of the South China Sea but also of the Indo-Pacific Region, China announced the *Belt Road Initiative (BRI)* in 2013, which has been discussed in Chapter 4 of the book.

After the promulgation of the *East Asia Strategy*, some of the first defence deals that USA did in the Indo-Pacific Region were the LEMOA in 2016, and the COMCASA in 2018 with India, which were consequent to the visit of the US President Barack Obama to India in January 2015 during which the two nations signed the "US-India Joint Strategic Vision for the Asia-Pacific and the Indian Ocean Region".

On one hand the US–India partnership was getting stronger and on the other hand, China's BRI scheme was gaining traction and notably the China–Pakistan relationship was getting deeper.

In 2015 and 2024, China ushered in the military reforms which had the latent objective of taking on its two main adversaries—the USA and India, for it has its eyes set on annexing Taiwan and Arunachal Pradesh. China's 2015 and 2024 military reforms too have been discussed in Chapter 4 of the book.

In 2012, Geoffrey Hinton demonstrated the power of Deep Learning, a subset of Machine Learning. Deep Learning Algorithms is regarded as the biggest scientific breakthrough since the nuclear weapons and the Internet in the 20th Century. The Chinese quite understood the importance of Artificial Intelligence (AI) in not only the day-to-day activities of the future, but its colossal importance in the weapon systems.

July 2017 saw China releasing the *New Generation Artificial Intelligence Development Plan* with the aim of becoming the global leader in AI by 2030. This shook the USA and India who now knew that China meant business and China's supremacy in warfare was certain if its AI dream were to be fulfilled.

To fulfil its AI dream China's needs high-technology semiconductors. Semiconductors are an essential component of electronic devices, defence equipment, healthcare, communications, computing, transportation and numerous other applications. In fact, in today's world, there is hardly anything that does not have a semiconductor in it or a semiconductor is used in its manufacturing. A semiconductor is an indispensable part of one's life today, knowingly or unknowingly.

Taiwan produces 50% of the world's semiconductors, while the USA and China produce just 12% and 7.6% respectively. Taiwan produces over 90% of the world's high-technology chips, thus making it a semiconductor superpower with no rivals visible on the horizon.

To become a world leader in semiconductor production by 2030, China has planned to build 31 semiconductor factories over four years commencing 2024, but the USA has put a spoke in the Chinese wheels.

On August 09, 2023, the US President Joe Biden signed the CHIPS and Science Act passed by the US Congress earlier in July 2023. This act entails giving more than US$ 50 billion in federal grants to firms building semiconductor manufacturing facilities in USA with a caveat not to upgrade any China-based factories for a decade. This created rumblings in China as it saw its semiconductor dream being dashed.

To further rub salt to the wounds of China was the lunch meeting of the US Speaker Nancy Pelosi with Morris Chang, the Founder, and Mark Liu, the Chairman of the Taiwan Semiconductor Manufacturing Company (TSMC) respectively on August 03, 2022 during her whistle-stop trip to Taiwan.

TSMC is the biggest chipmaker in the world with a market cap of over US$ 426 billion. TSMC intends to build a semiconductor facility in Arizona, USA, and would greatly benefit by the US CHIPS and Science Act.

Currently TSMC chips are used in the US F-35 fighter jets and Javelin missiles, apart from a plethora of the US military inventory that they are used in. With six of the world's top ten arms manufacturing companies located in the USA, it overscores the importance Taiwan has for the USA.

With three of the world's top ten arms manufacturing companies located in China, the desperation of China to be a reckonable global player in the semiconductor industry is well understood too.

However, China soon countered the US CHIPS and Science Act with its US$ 148 billion package in December 2022, with the aim of bolstering China's indigenous semiconductor industry. Its AI Dream is back on track.

And on August 29, 2023, Huawei, a leading Chinese multinational digital communications conglomerate, announced the manufacturing of the semiconductor chip Kirin 9000S. Thus, ensuring that China's dream to becoming the global leader in AI by 2030 continues undeterred.

Pakistan and China's friendship which had reached dizzy heights during Xi Jinping's visit to Pakistan in 2015, during which the CPEC was signed, moved few more notches up as the time passed by. Since 2021, Pakistan Army officers are being posted to the Western Theatre Command of China, an unheard thing amongst foreign armies. Though officers and soldiers do military exercises in foreign countries and attend courses of instructions, but never before in military history have officers been posted in a foreign country's military headquarters. This shows the trust and bonding that the PLA and the Pakistan Army have in each other, which is warning bells for India.

The same year, in 2021, a direct Optical Fibre Cable was laid between the Western Theatre Command of China in Chengdu and the GHQ of the Pakistan Army in Rawalpindi for swift and uninterrupted communications. Apart from this, Pakistan and China have been regularly holding joint army, maritime and air exercises where the aspect of interoperability of each other's weapon systems is given weightage so that when the need arises, the Pakistani troops can man PLA's weapon systems and vice versa.

On March 20, 2023, China completed the construction of the biggest naval submarine base in South Asia by constructing it in Cox Bazar in Bangladesh, Thus, with Gwadar port in Pakistan and Hambantota port in Sri Lanka firmly in the Chinese grip and with huge interests in Cox Bazar, the planning of China to encircle India by the sea route is complete. Also, Chinese military activity has been noticed in Laamu Atoll in Maldives and Kyaukphyu in Myanmar, which are clear signs of Chinese military activity in the Arabian Sea and the Bay of Bengal. The *String of Pearls* under which India is being encircled by the sea route has been discussed in detail in Chapter 4 of the book.

As the modernisation of the PLA is to be completed by 2027 and the huge quantum of two aircraft carriers, 21 nuclear submarines and 200 warships that are to be completed by China in 2030, coupled with the infrastructure development of Xinjiang and Tibet slated to be completed by 2032, and the production of 1,500 nuclear warheads by 2035. Clearly these huge military preparations by China aren't for a party or picnic but for something serious, and it is to annex Arunachal Pradesh, and all the timelines are pointing towards the impending war.

According to the 2024 Annual Threat Assessment released on February 05, 2024, by the Director of National Intelligence, USA, since the relations of India with both China and Pakistan are fragile, it is likely to result in a war between these three nations.

China is ahead of India by three decades in military preparedness.

Gen MM Naravane (Retd), the 28th Chief of Staff of the Indian Army who retired in 2022, in an article in *The Print* a well-known Indian publication, on August 07, 2023, has written that a two-front war would mean defeat.

The warnings bells for India have started chiming and the threat this time is from the two nations jointly, with whom India has fought wars one-to-one in different sectors and in different years earlier. But the next war that India will fight will be against China and Pakistan combine, and all timelines point to 2035.

8

Countering China

In the preceding seven chapters of the book, the rise of China both economically and militarily has been discussed, along with the three wars that it will wage from 2027 to 2035. While at the time of writing this book, the odds are weighed heavily in favour of China in the three wars it will wage for Taiwan, Spratly Islands and Arunachal Pradesh in India, but all is still not lost. There is no problem in the world—how complex and complicated it may be—for which a solution doesn't exist. There is no adversary, however mighty and muscular it may be, which can't be defeated in any sphere of life or in war, provided the defender knows where to strike, how to strike and more importantly, when to start striking.

The time to strike China is now or never. With each passing year, China is getting economically and militarily stronger because of three pivotal reasons: one party political system, keeping religion within the four walls of a house, and implementation of policies in a strict time frame.

If China wins these three wars which have been discussed in Chapter 5-7 of the book, the next three wars that will fought by China post the two-front war with India, will be discussed in the sequel to the book to be published around 2035. It will be much easier for China to win the three wars post-2035, because of the battle experience that it would have gained in waging the three wars for Taiwan, Spratly Islands and Arunachal Pradesh in India.

And the day China wins all these six wars, it will spell disaster for democracy and rules-based world order. To curb and contain China, so that China's checkmate doesn't become successful, no rocket science is needed and neither are complex and complicated mathematical equations needed. What is needed is the understanding of China's designs which have been discussed in the previous seven chapters of the book and measures given in this chapter that can nought China's checkmate.

Global Trade with China Needs to be Curtailed

It is ironic that even as the threat of China is being voiced by some quarters in the last over one decade of Xi Jinping being the Paramount Leader and President of China since March 2013, the global trade with China has been increasing year-on-year (YoY). Even the dreaded Covid-19 pandemic, which struck the world at the end of 2019 and raged until the end of 2022, resulting in over 7 million deaths being reported worldwide, the origins of which are stated to be in Wuhan, China, the global trade with China has increased YoY since 2020 onwards.

In 2021, the global trade of China was worth US$ 6.05 trillion, up 43.3% from 2020. In 2022, the global trade of China increased to US$ 6.25 trillion, up 7.7% from 2021. The next year, 2023, did see a slight decline of 5% in the global trade with China, with the figures pegged at US$ 5.94 trillion. Though on face value it was something to cheer at the start, but digging deeper it brought out more concern as China sensing the global outrage against for Covid-19 pandemic, had smartly invested heavily in firms in countries like Mexico and Vietnam, who were now supplying items without the risk of being labelled as "Made in China". The exact figures of such an indirect trading practise adopted by China to circumvent the global outrage of the Covid-19 outbreak will never be known, but clearly, directly or indirectly, China still remains the global manufacturing hub.

Part of every dollar traded with China is helping in strengthening the PLA. With such whopping global trade figures of China, it is no surprise that China has increased its defence budget in 2024 for the ninth consecutive time. China's 2024 Defence Budget announced at the 14th National People's Congress on March 12,

2024, saw a 7.2% increase over the preceding year, with the defence budget at US$ 231.4 billion. Interestingly, China's defence budget has more than doubled since 2015. A point to reiterate here is that Xi Jinping became the Paramount Leader of China in 2013.

In comparative terms, China's defence budget is twelve times the defence budget of Taiwan and thrice more than India's defence budget of US$ 75 billion. Clearly, the path of PLA's modernisation to be completed by 2027 is on track and will not suffer due to budgetary constraints as is the case with many of China's adversaries.

The India–China trade too has been increasing YoY. In 2020, the India–China trade was worth US$ 87.65 billion. The *Galwan Valley Clash* happen on June 15, 2020, in which 20 soldiers of the Indian Army were killed in action fighting the PLA. Despite this, India's trade with China soared to US$ 125 billion in 2021 and US$ 135.98 billion in 2022. In 2023, the India–China trade stood at an all-time high of US$ 136.2 billion.

While it is understandable that since most nations are members of the World Trade Organisation (WTO) and hence have to abide by the WTO resolutions and policies, and hence can't put a blanket ban on import from any specific country. It is the businessmen, who should realise that by importing from countries who have war designs on their own countries, are strengthening the armies in an indirect manner. Hence, rather than importing from these countries, alternative methods should be resorted to like importing from friendly countries or manufacturing products domestically.

A case study that can be emulated globally is the *Atmanirbhar Bharat* (Self-reliant India) and the *Make in India* initiatives launched by India.

In the period 2009–2013, India was the biggest arms importer in the world with a 14% share in the arms imports worldwide, up from 7% in the period 2004–2008.

Few months after being elected as the Prime Minister of India, Narendra Modi in September 2014, for the first time launched the *Make in India* initiative which was buttressed by the slogan of *Atmanirbhar Bharat* (Self-reliant India) on May 12, 2020.

Make in India and *Atmanirbhar Bharat* soon became the guiding mantra for the Indian entrepreneurs and the common citizen, which also inspired the dormant Indian arms industry, whose exports were just worth US$ 82 million in 2013–14.

Indian arms exports saw a phenomenal leap to US$ 1.93 billion in the year 2022–23 and are expected to touch US$ 15 billion by 2026–27.

India is now manufacturing warships, submarines, light combat aircrafts, utility helicopters and field guns to name a few, amongst the large defence inventory that is heralding India amongst the top arms manufacturing nations in the world.

From a decade back when India imported most of its defence requirements, today it is exporting arms in a big way which clearly shows the turnaround in this sector. The Service Headquarters of Indian Army, Indian Air Force, and the Indian Navy too have chipped in to this gigantic effort by constantly encouraging the Indian arms industry by making General Staff Qualitative Requirements (GSQR) simpler, so as to enable the domestic defence start-ups to also participate in the tendering process.

India today exports arms to 85 countries and is among the top 25 arms exporters in the world, ranked at 23. The Indian arms industry is currently valued at over US$ 8.2 billion.

Thus, India has turned the tables from being an arms importer to being an arms exporter in less than a decade. The success shown by India in its domestic defence manufacturing industry needs to be emulated across all sectors and in this endeavour, the entrepreneurs now need to take the lead, even at the cost of lesser profits as compared to importing from China.

However, there is a catch that despite the success in India's domestic defence manufacturing sector, India was still the world's biggest importer of arms during the period 2019–23 according to a report published by the reputed Swedish think-tank Stockholm International Peace Research Institute (SIPRI) on March 13, 2024. The imports of arms by India went up by 4.7% during the period 2019–23 as compared to the period 2014–18.

One of the main reasons for high imports by India is that the imported defence technology is exorbitantly expensive, as the Indian in-house Research & Development (R&D) is very weak compared to China. To develop world-class defence technology in any country, R&D plays the pivotal role and for this more doctorates in fields like Science, Technology, Engineering and Mathematics (STEM) are needed, for these four fields are the backbone of any Research & Development which takes place worldwide.

To achieve this, a nation needs to have world-class universities which rank very high in the global ranking order as the best brains of the world flock to such universities as faculty, which are ranked high in the global ranking order.

In 2015, Xi Jinping announced *World Class 2.0* project in which he wanted to have at least two Chinese universities in the world's top 500 by 2030, as none were in the top 500 list at that time. China hired the best brains of the world with good pay packages, and as of 2023 China has two universities in the top ten in the world. To hire the best brains, a nation also needs to ensure that the pay packages of these faculty are of global standing because only then will such people come to teach in a country. Once this is achieved, the R&D will see a significant change. As a result, more defence technology will be produced within a country rather than relying on any foreign country for transfer of technology.

R&D plays a major role in a country becoming a manufacturing hub, apart from business-friendly laws, low taxes and skilled manpower. The world's two biggest manufacturing hubs i.e. China and the USA are also the world's two top nations in having the largest PhDs in STEM. In 2019, China produced 49,498 PhDs in STEM, and the USA produced 33,759 whereas India produced about 700 PhDs in STEM.

By 2025, China is projected to have 77,179 STEM PhDs which would be nearly double of the 39,959 projected STEM PhDs of the USA the same year. This issue has been discussed in detail in Chapter 4 of the book.

The figures for spending on R&D also show startling facts. According to a study conducted by the Indian government think-tank *Niti Aayog* in 2022, while USA spent 2.9% of its GDP on R&D, China spent 2% of its GDP, and India spent 0.7% of its GDP on R&D in the period 2017–18.

Clearly, both for the USA and India, who are the main adversaries of China need more R&D spending on a war footing and more STEM PhDs needs to be encouraged.

The global citizen needs to avoid purchasing any Chinese products, however cheap and cost-effective they may be. Though, it is easier said than done, as out of ten products available off the market shelf today, nine are Made in China!

The challenges to reduce trade with China are enormous, but if a beginning is made by each and every global citizen, it will have a cascading effect. Until China's economic grip on the world is not weakened, the PLA will keep getting stronger.

Hike in Defence Spending

The nations that are to go to war in the coming years with China like Taiwan, India, the Philippines, Vietnam, Japan and South Korea, need to increase their defence budgets, because given the present defence budgets of these seven nations— which are to go to the three wars with China in the period up to 2035— is grossly inadequate to match the combat power of China as on date.

Compared to China's defence budget of US$ 231.4 billion for 2024, India has a defence budget of US$ 75 billion, Taiwan has a defence budget of US$ 90.9 billion, Japan has a defence budget of US$ 55.9 billion, while the Philippines, Vietnam, and South Korea have defence budgets pegged at US$ 4.1 billion, US$ 7.9 billion, and US$ 45 billion respectively for 2024.

While it is understandable that countries like India, Vietnam, and the Philippines are developing countries and need money for other developmental schemes, but the question is of national security, which is at stake for these countries due to the aggressive and assertive designs being exhibited by China. Nothing, whatsoever, can override a country's national security and now clear signs are visible on the horizon of the impending wars to be waged by China.

The USA which will get involved directly, if it decides to do so, in the first two wars that China will wage for Taiwan and the Spratly Islands already has a defence budget of US$ 886 billion, which is nearly four times the defence budget of China.

The USA has, in fact, reduced its defence budget from US$ 916 billion in 2023 to US$ 886 billion at a time when China's war for Taiwan is slated in 2027. Hence, the USA needs to ramp up its defence budget if China's war designs for Taiwan and Spratly Islands are to be countered, as both the wars are not too far away.

In the next decade, till 2035, if the seven nations who are to face China's aggression namely the USA, Taiwan, India, the Philippines, Vietnam, Japan and South Korea can increase their combat power and combat potential it will be a strong deterrence to China. And if these three wars of China for Taiwan, Spratly Islands and Arunachal Pradesh are not allowed to take place, the remaining three wars by China will not happen as a strong military deterrence is what will keep China at bay.

Strong military deterrence will only be built up when adequate defence budgets are allocated to the respective militaries of these seven nations who will fight the PLA in the times ahead.

India's defence budget of US$ 75 billion, which is 1.89% of the GDP, needs to be increased to at least 3% of the GDP annually till 2035 so that it enhances its military prowess to tackle the threat of the two-front war of China and Pakistan. As stated in Chapter 7 of the book, China is three decades ahead of India in military preparedness. And if the combat power of Pakistan's military is added to China's military capabilities, the balance tilts more in favour of the China and Pakistan combined.

For the Indian military to be capable of taking on the offensive by both China and Pakistan in tandem, increased defence budgets will help bridge the three-decade lead that the PLA has over the Indian Armed Forces, for just 11 years are left till 2035.

For those peaceniks who say that war will not happen in the future, should know that at the time of writing the book there are 13 wars and conflicts going on the world over including the two famous wars of Russia–Ukraine and Israel–Hamas.

Till the world and humanity will exist, wars can never end. A strong defence budget will vastly increase military deterrence and there are no shortcuts to this.

Artificial Intelligence in Weapons

Way back in 1999, when computers were still not common and smartphones were unheard of, China launched the *Beijing Key Laboratory of Human-Computer Interaction*. The same year the Shanghai-based *International Mesoscopic Connectome Project* was unveiled as part of the Chinese Academy of Sciences' Institute of Neuroscience. These two projects were the initial initiatives of China to bring about a cohesion in human and artificial intelligence.

In 2006, China issued the *National Medium and Long-term S&T Development Plan*, which earmarked brain science and cognition amongst its top research priorities. However, AI as a stand-alone discipline in China made its maiden appearance in the PRC State Council notification No. 40 issued on July 01, 2015 titled *State*

Council Guiding Opinions on Positively Promoting 'Internet +' Activity".

In March 2016, China announced the *China Brain Project*, which was to be a 15-year effort that would prioritise brain-inspired AI over other approaches. Moving ahead, on July 08, 2017, China announced the *New Generation AI Development Plan* which aimed to advance AI development in China in three stages with the final aim of China becoming the world leader in AI by 2030.

By the time the Russian President Vladimir Putin remarked on September 04, 2017, that the nation that leads in Artificial Intelligence (AI) will be the ruler of the world, China was already galloping ahead in the AI world.

It has already been explained in Chapter 7 of the book that the CHIPS and Science Act promulgated by the USA to stop China from manufacturing the semiconductors which are important in achieving AI superiority has failed to stop China's march as the global AI leader by 2030.

Since the future wars to be waged from China will have AI-embedded weapons which will play havoc when unleashed as they will have in-built decision-making capabilities in nanoseconds, it is important that modern weapons being manufactured by other leading arms manufacturers like the USA, Germany, France or India have a high degree of AI incorporated in them.

On August 28, 2023, cognizant of China's growing capabilities in AI, the US Department of Defence Deputy Secretary, Katheleen Hicks, announced the setting up of the *Replicator Programme* for the US military that will have all-domain autonomous systems and is to be completed in 18–24 months. Clearly, the 2027 timeline of China's war for Taiwan is weighing heavily on Pentagon. Kathleen Hicks while announcing the *Replicator Programme* at a defence technology conference in Washington, has touted this project as "a big bet". No doubt the stakes for USA over China's war for Taiwan are immensely high.

India is currently ranked 15th among the world's top 25 AI nations, with the pole position at the moment with the USA, though China isn't too far behind at second position. India hosted the 2023 summit of the *Global Partnership on Artificial Intelligence*, which was held on December 12–14, 2023 in New Delhi, thereby signalling its serious intent for development of AI, whose importance can't be underscored more in modern warfare.

India on February 29, 2024, announced US$ 11 billion worth of three projects to set up its maiden semiconductor fabrication plant and two assembly units in collaboration with Taiwan, Japan and Thailand.

Things have started moving but the speed needs to pick up as it is a race against time, with China well poised to become the global leader in AI by 2030.

Enhanced Space Warfare Capabilities

Mao Zedong in the late 1950s, decided to invest in long-range missiles and space technology despite the fact that, at that time, China was a poor country, just few years after having undergone a civil war. Qian Xuesen is regarded as the "Father of Chinese Rocketry", who studied science in the Massachusetts Institute of Technology, and the California Institute of Technology, both located in the USA.

Having gained on-hands experience by working on the USA's *Manhattan Project* to develop the first atomic bomb, Qian Xuesen had an unceremonious exit from the USA to China in 1955 after being arrested in the USA for few years on charges of being a Communist sympathiser after the Communists seized power in China at the end of the Chinese Civil War in 1949.

Qian Xuesen's parting words to the reporters while leaving the USA for China after his release in 1955 were that he would never set foot on the American soil. He lived up to his word and as time would reveal in an ironical twist of fate, he propelled China in reckoning to overtake the USA as the global space power.

Former US Navy Secretary Dan Kimball remarked that America's treatment of Qian was "the stupidest thing the USA ever did". He was absolutely correct as the USA would pay a heavy price for this act of ill-treating Qian Xuesen.

In April 1970, China became the fifth country in the world to put a satellite in orbit after the USSR, the USA, France and Japan. And in 2003, China became the third country in the world to send a human in space after the USA and the USSR.

But what shook the world was China deliberately destroying one of its own weather satellites in 2007 in a space bound missile test known as *Kinetic Kill Vehicle* (KKV). And what send more shockwaves globally was that the KKV, travelling at 29,000 kilometres/hour, with just a second to go before impact, made three lightning-quick adjustments to its trajectory to hit the two-meter-long satellite head-on.

By demonstrating the KKV in 2007, China had arrived as a reckonable global space power.

Deterred by China's foray into space warfare, the USA in 2011 passed the *Wolf Amendment*, limiting the ability of National Aeronautics and Space Administration (NASA) to cooperate with Chinese organisations and citizens. Subsequently, China has been frozen out of *Artemis Accords* which is a treaty seeking to govern space exploration.

Undeterred China started forming strategic scientific relationships with other countries and building a domestic space industry far more superior and bigger than the USA could ever imagine.

On June 23, 2020, the final satellite of BeiDou Navigation Satellite System was put into orbit to challenge the American-owned Global Positioning System (GPS). BeiDou which was launched on October 31, 2000, is the global navigation satellite system which does not require the user to transmit any data and operates independently of any telephonic or internet reception. It has satellites operating in three different orbits, including 24 satellites in medium circle orbits (covering the world), three satellites in inclined geosynchronous orbits (covering the Asia-Pacific Region), and three satellites in geostationary orbits (covering China).

The Beidou-3 (third-generation BeiDou) Navigation Satellite System became fully operational in July 2020, and earlier in 2016 itself had reached millimetre-level accuracy with post-processing.

And on May 14, 2021, China landed the Zhurong rover on Mars, becoming the third country in the world to successfully soft-land a spacecraft on Mars, following the footsteps of the USA and the USSR.

On January 28, 2022, China published a white paper on its space programme called *China's Space Program: A 2021 Perspective*, whose first paragraph has a quote by Xi Jinping "To explore the vast cosmos, develop the space industry, and build China into a space power is our eternal dream".

On January 10, 2024, Nikkei Asia, a globally reputed publication reported that China was building a satellite internet constellation using low Earth orbit in 2024 and plans to launch 26,000 satellites to cover the entire world.

And to put all speculations to rest of any doubts of China's space prowess, General Stephen Whiting, the Commander of the US Space Command stated on April 24, 2024, "Frankly, the People's Republic of China is moving at breath taking speed in space, and they are rapidly developing a range of counter space weapons to hold at risk our space capabilities".

Though various reports published in 2022 suggest that China will overtake the USA as the world's leader in space in 2045, however, going by the strides China has made in space power in the last two years, China will overtake the USA as the global space power by 2035 as that year is very critical and crucial for China for it has to wage a joint two-front war with Pakistan on India. This 2035 war will be the last war that Xi Jinping will be overseeing due to his age factor. Hence, all stops will be pulled by China overtake the USA in this field since space will have an important bearing on modern wars.

The US 2022 Nuclear Posture Review released on October 27, 2022, has stated that the speed with which both China and Russia are increasing their nuclear arsenals, by the 2030s USA will face two major nuclear powers as strategic competitors and potential adversaries. The report further mentions China's increasing nuclear capability as a threat to the United States and allies.

Where does India stand in the global space power race? According to the *Military Balance* report released in February 2024 by the International Institute of Strategic Studies, London, while China operates 245 military satellites, India has 26.

What is equally worrisome for both the USA and India, the two big nations to face China in the three wars up to 2035 though at different timeframes, is that in 2018, Lt Gen Robert Ashley, the Director of the US Defence Intelligence Agency, warned that China was working on the ability to jam satellites from the ground. Given how secretive China is, the result of this statement made six years ago will only be known in 2027 when China invades Taiwan.

A gigantic effort needs to be put by both the USA and India on a war footing to counter China's increasing space power which is both deadly and dangerous.

New Military Alliance

To contain the Chinese control of the Indo-Pacific region two important developments have taken place in the last fifteen years.

One is the initiation of the *Quadrilateral Security Dialogue* (QSD) colloquially called Quad, by the Japanese Prime Minister Shinzo Abe in 2007, with the support of the Australian Prime Minister John Howard, Indian Prime Minister Manmohan Singh and the US Vice President Dick Cheney.

The other is the formulation of the *Free and Open Indo-Pacific* strategy also known as the FOIP strategy or simply as the Indo-Pacific strategy, in 2016 by Japan, and the United States Department of State publishing it as a formalised concept on November 04, 2019.

Quad after its inception in 2007, was followed by a joint military exercise between the member nations on a grand scale called Exercise Malabar.

For a brief period, Australia withdrew from Quad when Kevin Rudd became the Prime Minister of Australia. In 2010 after Julia Gillard took over as the Prime Minister of Australia, it renewed its military relationship with the USA, which led to the deployment of the US Marines in Darwin, Australia, overlooking the Timor Sea and the Lombok Strait.

During the 2017 ASEAN Summit in Manila, Indian Prime Minister Narendra Modi, Japanese Prime Minister Shinzo Abe, Australian Prime Minister Malcolm Turnbull, and the US President Donald Trump agreed to revive Quad as it was imperative now to check the growing influence of China in the Indo-Pacific region.

A joint statement by the Quad members in March 2021, called "The Spirit of the Quad" was released which spoke of a shared vision for a FOIP and a rule-based maritime order in the East and South China seas.

With strong US naval bases in South Korea and Japan and with the emergence of Quad as a regional power, China knew that it had to act really fast in order to counter balance the near supremacy that Quad seemed to be enjoying.

Solomon Islands consists of six major islands and over 900 smaller islands and is located in Oceania. It has an area of 28,400 square kilometres and a population of 0.6 million. Solomon Islands has no armed forces, and the security of the island nation is looked after its police. The distance of Solomon Islands from China is 7,731 kilometres, but what is of paramount importance to China is the location of this island nation.

Solomon Islands is located 3,280 kilometres from Australia and with the growing stature of Quad, having good relations with Solomon Islands would serve two purposes for China.

Firstly, it gains an important foothold in the Oceania region to exert power over the Pacific Ocean by establishing an important naval base here in the near future. Secondly, it puts Australia at deterrence who is a member of Quad.

On April 20, 2022, Prime Minister Manasseh Sogavare of the Solomon Islands announced that his government had signed a security agreement with China. This announcement sent tremors across the entire world as now China had secured a foothold in the island nation which played a decisive role in World War II. China can now use this foothold to block shipping routes whenever the need arises.

China has agreed to pump in millions of dollars to boost up infrastructure in the island nation. Of course, there aren't any free lunches in the world. The takeover of Hambantota port in Sri Lanka, and the Gwadar port in Pakistan by China, for failure to repay the Chinese loans are a stark reminder what awaits Solomon Islands in the near future.

Australia which is located closer to Solomon Islands than China, pressurised the island nation to not sign the security agreement with China. But the decade long effort by China paid off, thus sending more shock waves throughout the world.

Even as the shock waves did not subside, Solomon Islands signed a Memorandum of Understanding (MoU) with a Chinese firm on April 30, 2022, to make a regional aeronautical hub in the island nation.

China has not accepted the formation of Quad gracefully and calls it Asian NATO. But since Quad is not a military alliance, so its efficacy during a war unleashed by China is extremely doubtful.

The time is now opportune to form a military alliance between the seven nations: the USA, Taiwan, India, the Philippines, Vietnam, Japan and South Korea which are to go to war with China in the next 11 years for two reasons. One, there is no military alliance that exists in the Indo-Pacific region amongst the countries that are facing the maximum threat due to China's ever increasing military power. Two, China only understands a strong military language, and these seven countries are incapable as on date to fight China single handedly.

Making International Organisations Accountable

As the Covid-19 pandemic raged across the world commencing in late 2019, one world body whose credibility came under the global scanner was the World Health Organisation (WHO). Founded on April 07, 1948, and headquartered in Geneva, Switzerland, with six regional offices and 150 field offices worldwide, WHO's official mandate is to promote health and safety while helping the vulnerable worldwide.

In the past WHO played a pivotal role in eradication of smallpox, the development of Ebola vaccine and near-eradication of polio. The WHO is governed by the World Health Assembly composing of 194 member states and has a budget of US$ 6.83 billion for 2024–25.

Funding for WHO takes place from two main sources: member states paying their assessed contributions and voluntary contributions. Assessed contributions are a percentage of a country's GDP and voluntary contributions are largely from member states, other UN organisations, intergovernmental organisations, and other sources.

In 2019, China contributed US$ 75.8 million in assessed contributions and US$ 10.2 million in voluntary contributions, while USA gave US$ 236 million in assessed contributions and US$ 656 million in voluntary contributions.

On January 23, 2020, the WHO emergency meeting was split on declaring the Covid-19 a Public Health Emergency of International Concern (PHEIC), as the final authority to declare a PHEIC rests with the WHO Director-General (DG), who for some strange reason decided to wait despite admitting that the Covid-19 was an emergency in China.

The WHO DG Dr Tedros Adhanom Ghebreyesus met Xi Jinping in Beijing on January 28, 2020, and praised China's top leadership for its openness in sharing the information related to the virus. The truth lay elsewhere. China had concealed the vital information of this virus when it first emanated in Wuhan, thereby putting humanity at risk.

On January 30, 2020, the WHO DG on return from his Beijing trip declared the Covid-19 as PHEIC. The damage had already been done. The delay had resulted in ten-fold increase of confirmed Covid-19 cases with 7,781 confirmed cases being reported from 18 countries.

On March 20, 2020, during the Munich Security Conference, the WHO DG yet again curiously praised China and bizarrely called upon nations not to limit travel of their citizens to China, when it should have been the other way around.

As the Covid-19 spread like wildfire worldwide, over 7 million persons died and an estimated US$ 8.5 trillion loss in the world economy, besides pushing more than 34 million people worldwide into extreme poverty.

And till date, not one person or country has been blamed, despite all the death and destruction caused by the Covid-19 pandemic.

Now, the UN has 17 specialised agencies which deal in different aspects ranging from children's fund, food, agriculture, health, and much more and all of them are in the tight grip of China. These 17 specialised agencies of the UN cover almost every important aspect of the world and human welfare, and China is a big player in all these apart from being a Permanent Five (P-5) member of the UN with veto rights.

Thus, on many occasions dreaded terrorists like Sajid Mir, who is based in Pakistan, accused in the 26/11 terror attacks in Mumbai, India, in which 166 people were killed and over 300 injured, has not been designated as a global terrorist by the UN despite best efforts by the USA and India as China uses its veto power. On March 12, 2024, India's Permanent Representative to the UN, Ruchira Kamboj, strongly condemned the countries that use their veto powers to block evidence-based terrorist listings at the United Nations Security Council (UNSC).

Major structural revamp is needed in the UN wherein countries like India with the world's largest population, and the world's fifth economy should be made a member of the UNSC. Which should be expanded from the present strength of 15 members and the power of veto of the P-5 nations: the USA, Russia, China, United Kingdom and France are done away with. It is indeed ironical that the UN which projects itself as a harbinger of democracy and rules-based world order, has no internal democracy and any proposal or resolution can be vetoed by any P-5 member.

Such moves of expanding the UNSC and doing away the veto power will vastly reduce China's grip on the international organisations.

China Discussion on Mainstream Media

Julius Ceaser's quote "Great things should be done without hesitation so that the feeling of danger would not weaken the courage and speed", well explains the hesitation most countries have in expressing the danger China poses to them in some form or the other. The hesitation stems from the deep pockets that China has, and isn't shy of using the enormous money power at its disposal, for anything that contributes even the smallest way possible in achieving the *China Dream*. The hesitation is a choice between money and the truth.

The media comprising the print, electronic and social media, can play an important part in raising awareness of the global dangers that will accrue, in case China's hegemonic designs get fructified.

The Paris-based World Association of Newspapers represents 18,000 newspapers with 2.7 billion people reading newspapers every day. The world has a population of 8.1 billion people, and approximately 5.4 billion people watch television. And 6.94 billion people use smartphones.

Now with this kind of a huge reach that all the three forms of media have, it is surprising that there are very few media outlets who print and broadcast articles and programmes respectively, of the threat China poses to the world order and world peace when the danger is lurking just around the corner.

Until maximum citizens are not made aware of the strong grip that China is slowly but surely tightening on all domains of civil life as well as military domains— the main backbone of China's strength which is money—and which comes out of the global trade will not get weakened. Until this backbone is not struck, other measures will prove futile, and for this, more and more awareness need to be generated.

The electronic media news channels can play an all-important role in the awakening of the common global citizen, as the news channels with vast reach have a footprint on the social media too in form of accounts on popular social media sites like X (formerly Twitter), YouTube, Instagram, and Facebook, as the programmes that are telecast on the electronic media are streamed on their social media accounts.

The author is on 60 Indian and International news channels for discussions and debates for various defence and geopolitical issues, but rarely has the threat of China been discussed.

In India, for example, Pakistan-bashing shows are often broadcast on the Indian news channels, as it gives good Television Rating Points (TRPs) which in turn get more advertising and rake in more revenue for the media houses apart from being good for electoral gains. However, the real threat China is rarely discussed on the Indian news channels.

India needs to understand clearly and unambiguously that China is the main threat, and Pakistan is just a subset of this main threat. Gone are the days when stand-alone wars were fought between India–Pakistan and India–China. The next war will be a two-front war between China and Pakistan on one side and India on the other.

The Indian print media publications do publish articles delving on the Chinese threat to India, but as has been explained earlier that the reach of electronic media with its footprint in the social media is manifold more times than the reach of the print media.

Hence, the electronic media the world over has an important responsibility now in educating the world of the grave threat that every nation in the world is facing, directly or indirectly, because of China's war designs and growing aggressiveness and assertiveness in every possible sphere and domain one can think of.

Curbing the Chinese Illicit Drug Business

In this book, so far, China's way up to becoming an economic power and world's manufacturing hub has been discussed which gives China *White Money* also known as *Legal Money* or *Legitimate Money*, that is known and accounted through official documents and transactions.

But what is not known to the public at large is the *Black Money* also known as *Slush Money* or *Blood Money*, which is generated through dubious deals with the illicit drug business being the largest contributor in this type of revenue generation, which is hidden from official records and registers.

Until the early 1980s, the two main sources of illicit drugs for the world were regions known infamously as *Golden Triangle* and *Golden Crescent*.

While the *Golden Triangle* consists of a large mountainous region of approximately 200,000 square kilometres comprising Northeast Myanmar, Northwest Thailand and North Laos, centred on the confluence of the Ruak and Mekong rivers, the *Golden Crescent* comprises the region located at the crossroads of Central, South and West Asia covering the mountainous peripheries of Afghanistan and Pakistan, extending into eastern Iran.

However, looking closely, the illicit drug business in China is not a recent phenomenon but has its roots dating back almost two centuries back when the *First Opium War* was fought from September 04, 1839 to August 29, 1842, and the *Second Opium War* was waged from October 08, 1856 to October 24, 1860, between China and primarily the United Kingdom and other countries.

Ironically, while the *First Opium War* and the *Second Opium War* were fought for the Chinese ban on the opium trade being supported by the British, as opium was Britian's single most profitable commodity trade of the 19th century, now China has emerged as the biggest illicit drug dealing nation ever since it opened its borders to trade and tourism in early 1980s.

China is now the world's biggest producer of precursor chemicals which are mandatory for the production of crystal methamphetamine, fentanyl, cocaine, and 3,4-methylenedioxymethamphetamine (MDMA) apart from growing cannabis, ephedra, and opium poppy on a massive scale.

Fentanyl overdose is the leading cause of death among young Americans since 2019. The precursor chemicals are transhipped from China to the Mexican drug cartels, who process and manufacture synthetic opioids and the finished product Fentanyl is then smuggled across the porous 3,145 kilometres long border between the USA and Mexico.

Such is the widespread use of Fentanyl amongst the youth of USA that 23% of the American youth fail in qualifying criteria for enrolment in the US military. Thus, it is scary that a conventional war does not inflict so many casualties as the illicit drugs are doing, both physical and fatal.

It is estimated that 4.1% of the global population is addicted to illicit drugs, with China as the top source for illicit drugs and the global revenue earned in 2023 due to sale of illicit drugs is US$ 650 billion, with the lion's share of this *Black Money* going to China.

China is clearly roaring its way to the bank, be it by way of being the world's manufacturing hub or the main source and supplier of illicit drugs. Whether *White Money* or *Black Money*, China has both of them aplenty.

The global illicit drug trade contributes to 30% of the global illicit economy.

India, apart from being located in one of the world's most turbulent geopolitically locations with its two belligerent neighbours, China and Pakistan, is also wedged between the three areas known for the largest illicit drugs production—China, the Golden Triangle, and the Golden Crescent.

Thus, it won't be overboard to say that India is located in the toughest geopolitical situation with an impending two-front war and an ever-increasing illicit drug menace.

India has an illicit drug trade worth US$ 5.362 billion, while around 100 million people are addicted to illicit drugs as on June 09, 2022. Fifteen years ago in 2007, 20 million Indians were addicted to illicit drugs. A five-fold increase in just fifteen years is worrisome.

War footing efforts need to be taken at every level, be it at the global level of the United Nations, the national levels of each nation and at the province/state level. As of now, the measures seem to be grossly inadequate which is evidently clear by the rapid rise of the illicit drug users and the enormous revenue being generated due to the illicit drug trade.

One striking observation is that rarely are the main kingpins of the drug cartels arrested and brought to justice. More often, only the low-level drug peddlers are arrested, and hence the illicit drugs trade thrives with impunity.

India-Specific Measures to Counter China

In this last section of the chapter as well as the book, India-specific measures to counter China's growing power will be discussed as it is the only country to whom no military assistance will be forthcoming by either superpower the USA or Russia, when a two-front war is waged by China and Pakistan on India in 2035.

The USA might still come to the military aid of Taiwan and the Spratly Islands as the fall of these two will result in the collapse of the *First Island Chain* and eventually the whole Indo-Pacific Region will be thrown open to China, but will not send any soldier for the assistance of India, because the loss of Arunachal Pradesh and Jammu and Kashmir will not in any way affect the trade of the USA.

Russia will not come to the aid of India in case of the future war because of two reasons. One, the Russia-Ukraine War has resulted in a *no-limit friendship* which was stated by the Russian President Vladimir Putin during his visit to China on February 04–05, 2022, just days before the outbreak of the Russia-Ukraine War, as Russia having been internationally isolated by the USA and the West, has now embraced China.

Two, ever since the USA and India started getting closer after the US President Barack Obama announced the *East Asia Strategy* on December 21, 2011, the relations between Pakistan and Russia have started deepening as Russia is using this new-found friendship with Pakistan as a counterbalance to the growing American relationship with India.

Maintaining Internal Order: In 1947, Aung San, a prominent politician of Burma (now Myanmar), had said that if Unity in Diversity of Burma is played with, Burma will sink in chaos. In 1962, the Military Junta seized power and did exactly contrary to Aung San's caution and started playing merry hell with Burma's Unity in Diversity. In 1989, Burma's name was changed to Myanmar in its pseudo-nationalistic endeavours. As the internal strife in Myanmar continued because of the Military Junta's playing with the Unity and Diversity of the country, China started taking advantage of the internal mayhem in Myanmar and started supporting various militant outfits. One of such militant outfits is the United Wa State Army which controls large swathes of land in which no soldier of Myanmar's army can dare enter. The country which has 90% Buddhist population and Buddhism is regarded as one of the most peaceful religions in the world, has now slipped into a civil war with the conditions having come to such an impasse that the Myanmar President Myint Swe declared on November 09, 2023, that Myanmar will be split if the violence doesn't stop.

India too is a land of Unity in Diversity like Myanmar, but a much bigger bouquet with 89 major and minor religions and 122 major languages and 1,599 other languages that are spoken across the length and breadth of the country. However, since independence in 1947, some Indian politicians have been misusing religion and exploiting linguistic diversities for electoral gains. These fault lines have been well utilised by China and Pakistan who see it as convenient and cost-effective means to weaken India internally, by sponsoring terrorism in various Indian states, be it in Punjab in the 1980s or the ongoing terrorism in Jammu and Kashmir and some northeastern states of India.

While electoral win being the main aim of any political party is well understood, but weakening the country for electoral victories is definitely not in order. There are thousands of other issues on which poll campaigning or poll speeches can be built upon, rather than cherry picking only religion, language, and caste issues.

Whole-of-the-Nation Approach in Containing China: It should be understood by every Indian citizen that blunting the threat of China to India isn't the responsibility of only the Government of India and the Indian Armed Forces. There has to be a whole-of-the-nation-approach to tackle the growing threat of China in which every citizen of India has a role to play in whatever capacity and capability. To do this, it is important that India should have a *National Security Strategy* in public domain where the threats to India are clearly and unambiguously spelt out. Silence is not an option anymore as the war clouds have already started darkening.

While having a *National Security Strategy* in public domain has many advantages, the main advantage that accrues is that every government department, the private sector, the media, and each citizen is aware of the threats facing India and accordingly the whole-of-the-nation approach comes into play, else the efforts are piecemeal with no synergy amongst all the pillars that make up a nation.

The more awareness is created for the threat that China is to India, the more will the nation be well-prepared to tackle this challenge that is just over a decade away, and a *National Security Strategy* will play an important role in achieving this.

Agnipath Scheme: Future wars to be waged by China will begin in non-kinetic mode and roll on to a kinetic mode, once success is achieved. With China well-ahead in all the six domains of war the future wars of China will begin with the three domains of cyber, electromagnetic spectrum and space and then the three traditional domains land, sea, and air will come into play. Thus, the importance of all these six domains of war is significant, at some stage or the other.

For the wars to be fought on land, sea, and air, however sophisticated the technology and weapon system may become, but what will finally matter is the soldier behind the weapon. It takes 8–10 years for a soldier to be experienced in the field he is in, especially the fighting arms and the supporting arms.

The Indian Army comprises the fighting arms, the supporting arms and the services.

The fighting arms in the Indian Army comprises of: the Infantry, Armoured Corps, and the Mechanised Infantry. The supporting arms comprise the Regiment of Artillery, Corps of Army Air Defence, Army Aviation Corps, Corps of Engineers, Corps of Signals, and the Intelligence Corps.

The services comprise the Army Service Corps, the Army Ordnance Corps, and the Corps of Electrical and Mechanical Engineers whose main task is to provide logistics to the army.

The cutting edge of the Indian Army are the three fighting arms comprising the Infantry, Mechanised Infantry and the Armoured Corps as these three arms have the first direct contact with an enemy in a war and amongst these three it is invariably the Infantry who always holds the ground even after the armoured and mechanised columns have over run an enemy territory.

The supporting arms and the services play an important role in the fighting arms making tactical gains in the battlefield.

Infantry comprises various Regiments like the Maratha Light Infantry, Rajput Regiment, Bihar Regiment, Sikh Regiment, Gorkha Rifles, Jat Regiment, Assam Regiment, and the Sikh Light Infantry which have fixed troop composition.

Infantry is also known as the Queen of the Battle. Like in the game of chess, all moves hinge around protecting the Queen, similarly the Infantry is the most important as on it depends the final outcome of a war.

The various regiments of Infantry are further divided in battalions. A battalion is also called a Paltan in the Indian Army. It is for the *Izzat* or the honour of his regiment and his Paltan (battalion) that an infantryman willingly sacrifices his life for the nation when the call of duty beckons so.

This is the true essence of regimentation which takes years to build and which has made the Indian Army the finest fighting force in the world. Contrary to the notions that the regimentation is a colonial legacy, the fact is that, it existed in India much before the British came to rule India.

History is replete with the tales of bravery of the intrepid Marathas of Chhatrapati Shivaji Maharaj, the valiant Tamils of the Chola Dynasty, the fearless Assamese of the Ahom Dynasty, or the courageous Sikhs of Maharaja Ranjit Singh.

The British realising the immense combat potential that regionalism could play in having a strong army, formally raised the present regiments of the Infantry of the Indian Army, retaining the intrinsic character of each one of them as they existed before.

The bonding in the regiments and the battalions of the Infantry is because of various factors like the language they speak, the region they belong to, the food they eat, the God/Deity they worship, and from all these factors flows out the war cry of the regiments, which every infantryman shouts when he does "Dhaava" (charges at the enemy in hand-to-hand combat) which is always the final stage of wresting a territory from the enemy.

War cry is an essential aspect of getting into combat as it gets the adrenaline pumping and brings the focus of the entire fighting unit to the impending task. Festivals in each battalion are celebrated with gaiety and fervour, which are common for the troops of the battalion. This leads to the strong bond of human relationships and bonhomie, which clearly reflect on the operational performance.

These factors have been lost sight of as it has been over 53 years since the Indian Army has been embroiled in a full-fledged war since the 1971 war. As few propagate the end of regimentation in the Infantry by adopting the All India-All Class system of recruitment for mixed troops under the recently announced Agnipath Scheme, it should be remembered that regimentation comprising fixed troop composition is the fabric of Infantry regiments. If the regional composition of the regiments is diluted, the regimental fabric will get weakened.

The All India-All Class system of recruitment for mixed troops which is being followed since Independence in 1947, till date did not affect the existing fixed troops composition of the Infantry and was limited to the new raisings after 1947.

India is a diverse country and the principle of unity in diversity has been inscribed and enshrined in the constitution. The unity in diversity needs to be strengthened for extricating maximum combat potential. The same should continue to followed as hither-to-fore as the regimentation has proved to be very effective and efficient. Robert Atkins quote is quite apt, "Don't fix what's not broken".

It is of paramount importance that the present demographic and regional design of the fighting arms is not tinkered with.

It should be remembered that the basic character of modern warfare will always remain unequal and will invariably be skewed towards the side which is fundamentally stronger. It is common to see in many Infantry battalions, the second and third generation soldiers serving in the same battalions as their forefathers. This infuses unmeasurable love for the battalion and the regiment, which is quintessential in winning a war.

The last recruitment in the Indian Army under the earlier 15-year mandatory service rules took place in 2019, just before the Covid-19 pandemic struck in early 2020.

India announced a new recruitment scheme for the enrolment of soldiers in the Indian Armed Forces called as the *Agnipath Scheme* on June 14, 2022, which entails the enlistment of 46,000 soldiers every year for a contractual period of 4 years and subsequent retention of 25% of them for the full service in the Indian Armed Forces.

The lot of soldiers recruited in 2019 will retire in 2034 (unless they rise in the promotional sweepstakes), and that year onwards, in each Infantry battalion, which has 900 soldiers, 225 soldiers will be long service soldiers, and 675 will be *Agniveers* (soldiers recruited under the *Agnipath Scheme*) of up to 4-year service.

Out of these 225 soldiers, approximately 100 will be in centralised roles in the battalion and rifle companies, thus leaving just 125 soldiers to handle the sophisticated weaponry in the Infantry battalions like ATGMs, Mortars and MMGs which require at least 8–10 years to master these weapons.

These 125 would also be the leaders at sub-unit level who would be expected to go into a battle with 675 Agniveers with 4-year service or less. This roughly translates into an infantry section going into war with seven Agniveers and three experienced soldiers with considerable experience. If regimentation of fixed troop composition is done away with, such an infantry section's performance in war raises deep and serious questions.

The service of the 4-year period of an Agniveer will be grossly inadequate to meet the operational requirements of an Infantry battalion, and if the regimentation of fixed troop composition is too done away within the Infantry, there will be an incalculable price to pay post the 2034 era when a two-front war will be waged on India by China and Pakistan.

Similar would be the case for Armoured Corps and the supporting arms, which are following the fixed troop composition as they too have sophisticated weaponry and equipment in them.

Some changes are needed in the retention percentage of the Agniveers after their 4-year service, to ensure that the combat potential of the Indian Armed Forces is not denuded.

Withdrawal of the Indian Army from CI Ops: The Indian Army for long now has been deployed in the Counter Insurgency Operations (CI Ops) with major deployments being in Jammu and Kashmir and some northeastern states.

The involvement of the Indian Army in quelling internal disorders in India started in the mid-1950s when it was for the first time called upon for CI Ops duties in Nagaland. Ever since, the Indian Army has remained in most of the northeastern states of India for CI Ops over prolonged and protracted durations of time.

The Indian Army was deployed in Punjab from 1983–1995 for CI Ops in Punjab, and since 1990 has been deployed continuously in Jammu and Kashmir for internal security.

The primary role of the Indian Armed Forces is to defend the country from external aggression. The other roles often assigned to the Indian Armed Forces, be it CI Ops or aid to civil authorities are secondary.

Prolonged periods of deployment in secondary roles weans away the combat preparedness and combat planning as the focus gets oriented for these secondary roles at the cost of the primary role, that is conventional war.

Though there is an alternate of field area and peace station tenures and postings for both at the levels of fighting units and the soldiers but peace station deployments with a plethora of administrative work leaves less time for conventional war preparedness. And since CI Ops tenures are counted as part of field area profiles, so no conventional war training can be done in field area tenures.

With a huge portion of the Indian Army deployed in Jammu and Kashmir and some northeastern states for CI Ops, the time for conventional war training is scant and scarce.

With a two-front war looming on the horizon, it is time that the Indian Army is withdrawn from CI Ops and focusses purely on the conventional war planning and preparedness.

The CI Ops duties should be handed over to the paramilitary forces and the state police forces, as during a conventional war, as it is the paramilitary forces and the state police forces who will have to take over the CI Ops.

In a report on how terrorist groups end published by the RAND Corporation, a highly credible US global policy think tank, on 30 June 30, 2008, highlighted that only 7% of the terrorists' groups ended by using military force, whereas 43% ended through political dialogues, 40% through effective policing, and 10% after the objectives of the terrorist organisations had been achieved.

The earlier the Indian Army is withdrawn from CI Ops and these duties are handed over to the paramilitary forces and the state police forces, the better it will be for all the stakeholders involved in CI Ops. The words of General Norman Schwarzkopf "The more you sweat in peace, the less you bleed in war", that adorns every training establishment of the Indian Army holds a much deeper meaning than ever before.

A case study wherein a nation's army thought they would never face a conventional war again but only low intensity conflicts is Israel, needs to be discussed in this context of the Indian Army's prolonged deployment in CI Ops.

After the decisive 1973 Yom Kippur War, which resulted in a victory for Israel, the Israeli Defence Forces thought that in future they would only fight low intensity conflicts against guerrilla and terrorist forces. The consequence of such a strategic mistake has heavily cost Israel, with the Israel-Hamas War still raging for over 10 months after starting on October 07, 2023.

For every nation's army, which has adversaries across its borders or seas, the threat of a conventional war will always remain, to negate such a possibility is nothing but suicidal, and to not be well-prepared adequately when the warning signs are glaring is fatal.

Sun Tzu's quote "Let your plans be dark and impenetrable as night, and when you move, fall like a thunderbolt", should be the guiding mantra for both the USA and India as China's war clouds have started darkening and the great Chinese checkmate has started fructifying.

List of Abbreviations Used

AI - Artificial Intelligence

BECA - Basic Exchange and Cooperation Agreement

BPTA - Border Peace and Tranquillity Agreement

BRI – Belt Road Initiative

CCP - Chinese Communist Party

CCRG - Central Cultural Revolution Group

CFL - Cease Fire Line

CI Ops - Counter Insurgency Operations

CMC – Central Military Commission

COMCASA - Communications Compatibility and Security Agreement

CRG - Cultural Revolution Group

DG - Director General

DGMO - Director General Military Operations

FDI – Foreign Direct Investment

GDP – Gross Domestic Product

GHQ - General Headquarters

GOC - General Officer Commanding

GSOMIA - General Security of Military Information Agreement

IAF - Indian Air Force

iCET - Initiative on Critical and Emerging Technology

KKV - Kinetic Kill Vehicle

LAC – Line of Actual Control

LEMOA - Logistics Exchange Memorandum of Agreement

LOC – Line of Control

Lt Gen - Lieutenant General

PAF - Pakistan Air Force

PHEIC - Public Health Emergency of International Concern

PLA - People Liberation Army

PLAAF - People's Liberation Army Air Force

PLAN - People Liberation Army Navy

POJK - Pakistan Occupied Jammu & Kashmir

PPP – Purchasing Power Parity

PSC - Politburo Standing Committee

R&D – Research & Development

SCS – South China Sea

SEZ - Special Economic Zone

SLOC – Shipping Lines of Communication

STEM - Science, Technology, Engineering & Mathematics

TSMC - Taiwan Semiconductor Manufacturing Company

UNCIP - United Nations Commission for India and Pakistan

UNCLOS - United Nations Convention on the Law of the Sea

UNMOGIP - United Nations Military Observer Group in India & Pakistan

USAF - United States Air Force

WHO - World Health Organisation

YoY - Year-on-Year

References

Chapter 1

Geographical - Geo Explainer: Gobi Desert by Victoria Heath – July 04, 2023

United States National Institute – Pakistan and the Himalayas by William H. Hessler – August 1954

PBS – Himalayas Facts – February 11, 2011

UNESCO – Karakorum-Pamir

Chapter 2

UNESCO – Mao's Last Revolution

Chapter 3

Office of the Historian – Milestones: 1945–1952

CEPR – China is the World's Sole Manufacturing Superpower: A Aine Sketch of the Rise by Richard Baldwin – January 17, 2024

Deccan Herald – What Really Made China the Manufacturing Superpower by TCA Ranganathan – July 16, 2023

Medium – How did China become a Manufacturing Superpower by Yogesh Upadhyaya – July 29, 2023

Chapter 4

Forbes – US Universities Fall Further Behind China in Production of STEM PhDs by Michael T. Nietzel – August 7, 2021

United States National Institute – China's Navy Could Have 5 Aircraft Carriers, 10 Ballistic Missile Subs by 2030 says CSBA Report by John Grady – August 18, 2022

References

YouTube Video of Sky News Australia – China to Build 21 Nuclear Submarines by 2030

The Diplomat – Predicting the Chinese Navy of 2030 by Rick Joe – February 15, 2019

The Sunday Guardian – China's Global Navy Eyeing Sea Control by 2030, Superiority by 2049 by Captain James E. Fanell (Retd) – June 13, 2020

The Interpreter – By the Numbers: China's Nuclear Inventory Continues to Grow by Amrita Jash – February 27, 2024

Arms Control – The Unknowns about China's Nuclear Modernization Program by Fiona S. Cunnigham – June 2023

Congressional Research Service – China Naval Modernization: Implications for US Navy Capabilities – Background and Issues for Congress – January 30, 2024

Organisation for Research on China and Asia – Key Chinese Shipyards by Eerishika Pankaj –July 6, 2022

The Times of India – To Counter China in Indian Ocean Region, India plans 175-warship Navy by 2035 by Rajat Pandit – September 18, 2023

China Power – How is China Expanding its Infrastructure to Project Power Along its Western Borders?

The Diplomatist – The Malacca Dilemma and Chinese Ambitions: Two Sides of a Coin by Navya Mudunuri – July 7, 2020

Pakistan Today – Minister Announces Completion of 36 CPEC Projects Worth $24 billion by Staff Report – January 1, 2024

Military Review – The Levels of War as Levels of Analysis by Andrew S. Harvey, PhD

Indian Defence Review – Six Wars China is Sure to Fight in the Next 50 Years by IDR News Network – February 27, 2022

JSTOR – Rich Country, Strong Army: China's Comprehensive National Security by Oliver Corff – January 1, 2018

Washington Post – US General Warns Troops that War with China is Possible in Two Years by Dan Lamothe – January 27, 2023

Reuters – Biden Vows 'to Protect' Country in State of the Union speech, Refers to China Balloon by Patricia Zengerle – February 8, 2023

International Institute of Strategic Studies – China's New Information Support Force – May 3, 2024

Centre for Air Power Studies – China's Military Reorganisation and Emergence of an Aerospace Force by TH Anand Rao – May 1, 2024

Reuters - How Hamas Duped Israel as it Planned Devastating Attack – October 10, 2023

The Economic Times – China's Electromagnetic Warfare Game-Changer: 'Nowhere to Hide' for Enemy Forces.

Chapter 5

The White House, Washington – Indo-Pacific Strategy – February 2022

BBC – China and Taiwan: A Really Simple Guide – January 8, 2024

Taipei Times – Taiwan in Time: The Admiral's Secret Plan by Han Cheung – September 23, 2018

Nippon – Legacy and Lessons of the Second Taiwan Strait Crisis by Fukuda Madoka – August 23, 2023

US Army War College – Chinese Army Building in the Era of Jiang Zemin by Andrew Scobell Dr.

Gateway House – The Upward Swing of Beijing's Military Industrial Complex by Sameer Patil

The Times of India – China on Track to be Ready for Taiwan Invasion by 2027: US – March 21, 2024

The Guardian – Taiwan Poll Shows Dip in US Trust Amid Growing Concern Over China by Chi Hui Lin – November 23, 2023

Chapter 6

China Power – How Much Trade Transits the South China Sea

Breaking Defence – New Chinese 10-Dash Map Sparks Furor Across Indo-Pacific: Vietnam, India, the Philippines, Malaysia by Colin Clark – September 1, 2023

International Maritime Organisation – United Nations Convention on the Law of the Sea

Energy in Asia – The Spratly Islands Dispute: Why is this Important? By Diana M. NGO October 13, 2011

Chapter 7

Press Trust of India – Be Prepared for 'Black Swan' Events, Expect the Unexpected: Army Chief to Force

University of Oxford – Why was British India Partitioned in 1947? Considering the Role of Muhammad Ali Jinnah

The Guardian – Kashmir Letters Cast Doubt on Claims Nehru Blundered by Agreeing Ceasefire by Anisha Dutta – March 8, 2023

The Guardian – Sixty Years of US Aid to Pakistan

Observer Research Foundation -The Kashmir that India Lost: A Historical Analysis of India's Miscalculations on Gilgit Baltistan by Kirti M. Shah – October 20, 2021

Economic & Political Weekly – Dhaka 1969 by Nusrat Sabina Chowdhury – January 17, 2024

The Print – The 3 Foundational Agreements with US and What They Mean for India's Military Growth by Snehesh Alex Philip – October 27, 2020

The Hindu – India has Lost Access to 26 out of 65 Patrolling Points in Eastern Ladakh, says Research Paper by Vijaita Singh – January 24, 2023

Ministry of External Affairs, India – 21st Round of India–China Corps Commander Level Meeting – February 21, 2024

The Week – India Needs a Dedicated Mountain Strike Corps to Tackle China by Pradip R Sagar – July 4, 2021

India.com – New Army Division for Possible Deployment in Eastern Ladakh Likely to be Raised This Year: Report by Joy Pillai – April 14, 2024

Brookings – The American Pivot to Asia by Keneneth G. Lieberthal – December 21, 2011

Office of the Director of National Intelligence – Annual Threat Assessment – February 5, 2024

The Print – Is India Ready for Pakistan–China threat? Two-Front War Would Mean Defeat by Gen MM Naravane (Retd) – August 7, 2023

Indiastat – Indian Defence Expert Foresees War Threats to India: Urges Strategic Shifts in Military Preparedness & Diplomacy – February 15, 2024

Taiwan Insight – India-Taiwan Relations: Right Time to Move Ahead – September 20, 2022

The Wire – 2020 Gave India a sharp Lesson on the Chinese Military. When Will Indian Generals Take Heed? By Pravin Sawhney December 11, 2020

Chapter 8

The Economic Times – China Maintains Defence Budget Despite Economic Travails – March 12, 2024

Sputnik News – Military Expert Credits 'Make in India' & 'Atmanirbhar Bharat' for Booming Arms Export by Pawan Atri – June 1, 2023

The Hindu – India World's Top Arms Importer Between 2019–23: SIPRI by Dinakar Peri – March 13, 2024

The Economic Times – India's R&D Spends Amongst the Lowest in the World: NITI Aayog Study by Anand JC – July 21, 2022

Statista – Countries with the Highest Military Spending Worldwide in 2023

Ongoing Wars and Conflicts 2024 by Rodolfo Delgado – January 12, 2024

China's "New Generation" AI-Brain Project by Wm. C. Hanans and Huey-Meei Chang

Defence News – Replicator: An Inside Look at the Pentagon's Ambitious Drone Program by Noah Robertson – December 19, 2023

NBC News – How China is Challenging the US Military's Dominance in Space by Courtney Kube and Dan De Luce – December 13, 2023

Nikkei Asia – China to Launch 26,000 Satellites, Vying with US for Space Power by Shunsuke Tabeta – January 10, 2024

Council on Foreign Relations – The WHO and China: Dereliction of Duty by Michael Collins – February 27, 2020

NDTV – "Doublespeak": India Questions Veto-Blocking of Terrorist Listings at UN – March 12, 2024

Congressman David Trone – China's Role in Illicit Fentanyl Running Rampant on US Streets – January 8, 2023

CNBCTV18 – Around 100 Million Indians Consume Drugs like Cocaine and Cannabis, says Narco Top Cop by Story Tailors – June 9, 2022

RAND – How Terrorist Groups End by Seth G. Jones and Martin C. Libicki – June 30, 2008

The State Council, People's Republic of China – China's Space Program: A 2021 Perspective – January 28, 2022

Financial Express – Agnipath Explained: The Key Factors for the Scheme to Succeed in the Indian Army – July 31, 2022

Index

Active Defence Doctrine, 60
Afghanistan, 3, 5, 38, 46, 48, 166
Africa, 31, 55, 56, 72, 100, 106
AI, 142, 143, 144, 153, 154, 155, 177, 184
Air, 14, 39, 60, 65, 80, 88, 89, 100, 121, 122, 171, 178, 181
Airland Battle Doctrine, 60, 61, 63, 85
Aksai Chin, 3, 126, 128, 129, 133, 135, 137, 139
Artificial Intelligence, 142, 153, 154, 155, 177
Arunachal Pradesh, 46, 47, 127, 128, 131, 133, 134, 137, 138, 139, 142, 145, 146, 152, 168
Asia, 5, 30, 31, 38, 46, 48, 53, 55, 67, 92, 125, 126, 141, 144, 157, 166, 168, 180, 182, 183, 184
Asif Ali Zardari, 52
Atmanirbhar Bharat, 148, 149, 183
Aung San, 169
Bangladesh, 56, 57, 105, 106, 120, 144
Bay of Bengal, 57, 104, 105, 144
Beijing, 4, 6, 8, 11, 12, 14, 15, 22, 23, 28, 38, 42, 138, 153, 162, 181
Belt and Road Initiative, 29, 30, 31, 35, 37
Bhutan, 2, 47, 48, 105, 130, 133, 134, 135, 138
Bohai Sea, 4, 10
Boluan Fanzheng, 22, 23, 24
BRI, 30, 31, 32, 51, 55, 56, 64, 72, 141, 142, 177

Business, 32, 165
CCP, 7, 8, 9, 13, 14, 15, 16, 22, 23, 24, 28, 29, 30, 31, 36, 41, 62, 64, 69, 73, 75, 77, 78, 89, 90, 177
Central Military Commission, 14, 37, 177
Chiang Kai-shek, 20, 69, 75, 77, 125
Chief of Army Staff, 104, 120, 121
China, 12, 13, 1, 2, 3, 4, 5, 6, 7, 8, 9, 10, 11, 12, 13, 14, 15, 16, 17, 18, 19, 20, 21, 22, 23, 24, 25, 26, 28, 29, 30, 31, 32, 33, 34, 35, 36, 37, 38, 41, 42, 43, 44, 45, 46, 47, 48, 49, 50, 51, 52, 53, 54, 55, 56, 57, 58, 59, 61, 62, 63, 64, 65, 66, 67, 68, 69, 70, 71, 72, 73, 74, 75, 77, 78, 79, 80, 81, 82, 83, 84, 85, 86, 87, 88, 89, 90, 91, 92, 93, 94, 95, 96, 97, 98, 99, 100, 101, 102, 103, 104, 105, 113, 114, 121, 124, 125, 126, 127, 128, 129, 130, 131, 132, 133, 134, 135, 136, 137, 138, 139, 140, 141, 142, 143, 144, 145, 146, 147, 148, 149, 150, 151, 152, 153, 154, 155, 156, 157, 158, 159, 160, 161, 162, 163, 164, 165, 166, 167, 168, 169, 170, 174, 176, 179, 180, 181, 182, 183, 184
China Dream, 29, 30, 37, 44, 50, 163
China Pakistan Economic Corridor, 31, 51
Chinese Civil War, 12, 16, 17, 18, 19, 23, 29, 47, 49, 69, 73, 74, 75, 124, 125, 155
Chinese Communist Party, 7, 10, 12, 69, 177
Chinese War Strategy, 59, 62
CIA, 65, 87

CMC, 14, 16, 29, 37, 41, 177
COAS, 104, 122, 123, 131
Colombo, 56
Commissar, 22, 41
Covid-19, 97, 135, 147, 161, 162, 173
Cox Bazar, 56, 57, 144
CPEC, 31, 51, 52, 53, 54, 55, 56, 144, 180
Cultural Revolution, 7, 8, 10, 11, 12, 15, 21, 23, 24, 28, 89, 131, 177
Cultural Revolution Group, 11, 177
Cyber, 40
Dalai Lama, 127, 138
Defence Budget, 147, 183
Deng Xiaoping, 9, 10, 15, 16, 17, 20, 21, 22, 23, 24, 25, 26, 28, 49, 89
Djibouti, 55, 72
Drugs, 184
East China Sea, 38, 45, 67, 71, 92, 93
First Taiwan Strait Crisis, 41, 78, 79, 82
Five Fingers of Tibet, 47, 48
Forces Goal 2030, 56
Four Asian Tigers, 77
Four Modernisations Programme, 21
Four Olds, 11
Fourth Industrial Revolution, 33
Full Spectrum Operations Doctrine, 61, 62, 85
Galwan Valley Clash, 46, 133, 134, 136, 137, 148
GDP, 25, 26, 30, 32, 49, 50, 76, 151, 153, 161, 177
General Manoj Pande, 104
General SHFJ Manekshaw, 120
General Zia-ul-Haq, 121

Gobi Desert, 1, 2, 179
Golden Crescent, 166, 167
Golden Triangle, 166, 167
Great Chinese Checkmate, 13, 18
Great Chinese Famine, 8, 9
Great Leap Forward, 8, 9, 18, 89
Great Western Development Strategy, 49, 50
Gulf War, 61, 85
Gwadar, 53, 55, 56, 57, 72, 105, 144, 160
Hamas, 62, 65, 86, 91, 153, 176, 181
Hambantota, 55, 56, 57, 72, 144, 160
Han, 4, 181
Henry Kissinger, 19
Himalayas, 1, 2, 130, 179
Hong Kong, 6, 14, 38, 63, 74, 77
Hu Jintao, 29, 36, 51, 61, 62
IAF, 115, 120, 177
India, 4, 11, 12, 2, 3, 19, 35, 36, 38, 42, 43, 45, 46, 47, 48, 52, 53, 54, 56, 57, 58, 59, 63, 64, 65, 86, 92, 100, 102, 103, 104, 105, 106, 107, 108, 109, 110, 111, 112, 113, 114, 115, 116, 119, 120, 121, 122, 123, 124, 125, 126, 127, 128, 129, 130, 131, 132, 133, 134, 135, 136, 137, 138, 139, 140, 141, 142, 144, 145, 146, 148, 149, 150, 151, 152, 153, 154, 155, 157, 158, 161, 163, 164, 165, 167, 168, 169, 170, 172, 173, 174, 176, 178, 180, 181, 182, 183, 184
Indian Air Force, 115, 123, 129, 149, 177
Indian Army, 11, 12, 46, 104, 111, 114, 120, 123, 124, 127, 128, 129, 131, 134, 136, 137, 140, 145, 148, 149, 171, 172, 173, 174, 175, 176, 184
Indian National Congress, 106, 107

Indian Navy, 44, 45, 57, 105, 120, 149
Indonesia, 30, 93, 94, 95, 98, 99, 105
Israel, 62, 63, 65, 86, 91, 113, 153, 176, 181
Japan, 23, 38, 43, 45, 67, 68, 69, 73, 78, 93, 151, 152, 155, 156, 159, 161
Jiang Zemin, 81, 82, 83, 85, 181
Jimmy Carter, 20
Joe Biden, 65, 143
K2, 5, 48
Karachi, 53, 112
Karakoram, 1, 2, 3, 49, 53
Kazakhstan, 30, 46
Kuomintang, 23, 36, 69, 73, 74, 75, 76, 77
Kyaukpyu, 57, 105
Laamu Atoll, 58, 144
LAC, 54, 104, 127, 132, 136, 137, 140, 177
Ladakh, 3, 46, 47, 127, 129, 135, 136, 137, 183
Lahore, 53, 107, 110, 122
Land, 4, 138
Language, 117
Li Keqiang, 52
Lin Bao, 12, 13, 14, 15, 16
Line of Actual Control, 54, 104, 132, 177
Line of Control, 54, 105, 178
Little Red Book, 11
Liu Shaoqi, 9, 10
LoC, 105
Macau, 6, 38
Made in China, 30, 32, 33, 34, 35, 147, 151
Mahatma Gandhi, 106, 107, 125
Make in India, 148, 149, 183

Malacca Dilemma, 51, 52, 54, 180
Malaysia, 93, 94, 95, 98, 99, 182
Maldives, 57, 58, 59, 72, 105, 144
Manmohan Singh, 158
Mao Zedong, 7, 8, 9, 10, 11, 12, 13, 14, 15, 16, 17, 19, 20, 23, 26, 41, 42, 47, 48, 89, 127, 155
Middle East, 31, 55, 56, 141
Military Industrial Complex, 33, 35, 83, 84, 181
Military Reforms, 35, 37, 62, 84, 87
Missiles, 43
Mohamed Muizzu, 58
Mongolia, 1, 6, 14, 38, 46, 49, 63
Moscow, 22
Mount Everest, 5, 47, 48
Mumbai, 57, 105, 106, 163
Muslim League, 106, 107, 118
Myanmar, 38, 47, 57, 59, 95, 105, 138, 144, 166, 169
Narendra Modi, 136, 149, 159
National High-end Foreign Experts Recruitment, 34
NATO, 60, 160
Nawaz Sharif, 52, 122
Nepal, 2, 47, 48, 105
Nuclear, 41, 43, 82, 83, 158, 180
One China, 20, 21, 69, 81, 125
Operation Desert Storm, 61, 85
PAF, 115, 120, 178
Pakistan, 2, 3, 38, 46, 49, 52, 53, 54, 55, 56, 57, 63, 72, 86, 103, 104, 105, 106, 107, 108, 109, 110, 111, 112, 113, 114, 115, 116, 117, 118, 119, 120, 121, 122, 123, 124, 133, 134, 142, 144, 145, 153, 157, 160, 163, 164, 165, 166, 167, 168, 169, 174, 178, 179, 180, 182, 183
Pakistan Air Force, 114, 115, 178

Pakistan Occupied Jammu & Kashmir, 53, 178
Paracel Islands, 94, 95, 96
Paramount Leader, 23, 28, 29, 36, 37, 42, 49, 51, 55, 61, 81, 82, 86, 88, 89, 90, 97, 121, 132, 133, 135, 147, 148
Pentagon, 36, 85, 154, 184
Philippines, 43, 67, 71, 92, 93, 94, 95, 96, 97, 98, 99, 100, 103, 151, 152, 161, 182
PLA, 12, 13, 16, 23, 35, 36, 37, 38, 39, 40, 41, 46, 48, 51, 54, 61, 62, 78, 79, 80, 81, 82, 84, 85, 86, 87, 88, 103, 104, 128, 129, 130, 131, 134, 136, 137, 140, 144, 145, 147, 148, 151, 152, 153, 178
PLAAF, 14, 39, 43, 63, 80, 100, 102, 178
PLAGF, 39, 63
PLAN, 39, 43, 44, 45, 46, 56, 63, 85, 95, 100, 102, 178
Political Work Department, 37, 41
R&D, 33, 34, 83, 84, 150, 151, 178, 184
Red Army, 22, 36, 39, 59
Red August, 11
Red Guards, 11, 12
Reform and Opening Up Policy, 22, 23, 24
Republic of China, 17, 19, 21, 30, 31, 36, 67, 69, 74, 79, 125, 157, 184
Research & Development, 83, 150, 178
Richard Nixon, 18, 19, 20, 49, 100
Russia, 11, 7, 38, 43, 46, 64, 65, 88, 91, 101, 153, 158, 163, 168
Sanzi Yibao, 9
Science, Technology, Engineering & Mathematics, 34, 83, 178
SCS, 92, 93, 94, 95, 96, 97, 98, 99, 100, 141, 178

Sea, 4, 38, 43, 56, 71, 72, 92, 93, 96, 97, 98, 104, 105, 144, 159, 178, 180, 182
Second Taiwan Strait Crisis, 79, 80, 83, 181
Senkaku Islands, 63
Seven Thousand Cadres Conference, 8, 9, 11
SEZ, 21, 178
Shanghai, 4, 6, 14, 15, 20, 21, 29, 38, 153
Shanghai Communique, 20
Shinzo Abe, 158, 159
Shipping Lines of Communication, 51, 178
SLOC, 51, 56, 178
South China Sea, 3, 38, 44, 45, 67, 71, 92, 93, 94, 95, 96, 98, 99, 100, 102, 141, 178, 182
South Korea, 45, 77, 151, 152, 159, 161
Soviet, 17, 19, 59, 80, 83, 119, 127
Space, 155, 156, 157, 184
Special Economic Zones, 21
Spratly Islands, 63, 91, 92, 94, 95, 96, 97, 98, 99, 100, 103, 146, 152, 168, 182
Sri Lanka, 55, 56, 57, 72, 105, 144, 160
STEM, 34, 35, 83, 150, 151, 178, 179
String of Pearls, 52, 54, 55, 57, 59, 144
Sun Tzu, 1, 28, 86, 176
Taiwan, 5, 19, 20, 36, 38, 43, 44, 46, 49, 63, 64, 65, 66, 67, 68, 69, 70, 71, 73, 74, 75, 76, 77, 78, 79, 80, 81, 82, 83, 84, 85, 86, 87, 88, 90, 91, 92, 93, 94, 96, 97, 98, 100, 101, 102, 103, 125, 142, 143, 146, 148, 151, 152, 154, 155, 158, 161, 168, 178, 181, 182, 183

Taiwan Miracle, 75
Taiwan Strait, 20, 36, 38, 43, 67, 70, 74, 78, 79, 80, 82, 84, 85, 86, 88, 92
Tajikistan, 3, 46
Taklamakan Desert, 1, 2
Third Taiwan Strait Crisis, 70, 80, 81, 82, 85
Three Red Banners, 9
Tibet, 5, 6, 23, 38, 41, 46, 47, 48, 49, 51, 54, 126, 127, 129, 130, 138, 139, 145
Tibetan Plateau, 2, 4, 5, 47, 48
Trade, 126, 147, 182
Tsinghua University, 28
Turkey, 58
UN, 65, 69, 70, 161, 162, 163, 184
United Kingdom, 14, 45, 48, 163, 166
United Nations, 69, 70, 76, 96, 111, 112, 113, 115, 163, 167, 178, 182
Unity in Diversity, 169
US Army, 59, 60, 181
US Military, 36, 60, 84, 184
US Navy, 44, 45, 79, 80, 81, 85, 95, 100, 102, 156, 180
USA, 7, 13, 18, 19, 20, 21, 25, 26, 28, 32, 33, 34, 35, 36, 42, 44, 45, 47, 48, 52, 60, 61, 65, 66, 67, 70, 71, 72, 75, 78, 79, 80, 81, 82, 83, 84, 85, 87, 88, 91, 92, 95, 100, 101, 102, 103, 113, 127, 135, 136, 140, 141, 142, 143, 145, 151, 152, 154, 155, 156, 157, 158, 159, 161, 163, 166, 167, 168, 176

USSR, 13, 14, 17, 19, 42, 71, 119, 120, 127, 156, 157
Vietnam, 3, 38, 93, 94, 95, 96, 97, 98, 99, 100, 103, 147, 151, 152, 161, 182
Vishakhapatnam, 57, 105
Vladimir Lenin, 22
Wakhan Corridor, 3
Warfare, 155, 181
Watergate Scandal, 20
Wenweipo, 63, 64
White House, 20, 100, 181
WHO, 161, 162, 178, 184
William Burns, 65, 87
World Bank, 32
World Class 2.0, 150
World Health Organisation, 161, 178
World Trade Organisation, 148
Wuhan, 147, 162
Xi Jinping, 28, 29, 30, 31, 32, 33, 34, 35, 37, 41, 42, 44, 50, 52, 53, 54, 55, 62, 64, 84, 86, 87, 88, 89, 90, 97, 102, 121, 132, 133, 134, 135, 136, 137, 144, 147, 148, 150, 157, 158, 162
Xi Zhongxun, 24, 28
Xinjiang, 2, 6, 38, 41, 42, 46, 47, 48, 49, 50, 51, 54, 127, 129, 145
Yellow Sea, 4, 38
Zhou Enlai, 11, 12, 15, 16, 21, 23, 78, 79, 126, 128, 129, 139

Lt Col. JS Sodhi (Retd) is a veteran of the Bombay Sappers, Corps of Engineers of the Indian Army, with over 21 years of distinguished service. He is a seventh-generation Indian Army officer and a third-generation Corps of Engineers officer.

He is an alumnus of the National Defence Academy, Khadakwasla, Pune, and the Indian Military Academy, Dehradun.

He is a civil engineer, having done his B.Tech. from the College of Military Engineering, Pune, and his M.Tech. in Structures from the Indian Institute of Technology, Kanpur. He has also done an MBA in project management and L.Lb. He is a diploma in both French and Russian foreign languages.

He has been part of a study team sponsored by the Government of India to study the tsunami that hit the Indian coast on December 26, 2004. He has been part of rescue and relief operations in the aftermath of the Bhuj earthquake that hit Gujarat on January 26, 2001.

He has been awarded the General Officer Commanding-in-Chief's Commendation Card and the Chief of Army Staff's Commendation Card.

He is now an international media personality whose articles and comments on defense and strategic issues are frequently published in 40 reputed Indian and international publications, and he often appears on 60 leading Indian and international television news channels, apart from many prestigious FM radio channels for discussions and talk shows.

He has been a panelist speaker in an international seminar on "From China's 20th National Party Congress Onwards," organized by the University of Nottingham, United Kingdom, on October 20, 2022 in the United Kingdom.

He has also been a speaker at various international and national conferences organized by Devi Ahilya Vishwa Vidyalaya, Indore; Aligarh Muslim University, Aligarh; Woxsen University, Hyderabad; Amity University, Noida; and Jesus & Mary College, New Delhi.

He is an awardee of the "Lifetime Achievement Award" for his work in electronic media and print media. He is also an awardee of the "Icon of the Year Award" for his contribution in the field of defense and strategic affairs.

He features in the World Book of Records, London, and in the India Book of Records for his articles in print media and news channel appearances. He is a TEDx speaker who gave a Ted Talk on "Self-Reliance and Hard Work Can Propel a Person to Greater Success".

He is Editor, Global Strategic & Defense News. The publication was awarded the "Most Credible Geopolitical Publication Award" in 2023.

www.ingramcontent.com/pod-product-compliance
Lightning Source LLC
LaVergne TN
LVHW091542070526
838199LV00002B/173